JEFFREY HUNT ART
FANTASY DIGITAL ARTIST

DIGITAL ART
CONTENT CREATION
ART BOOK AUTHOR

Copyright © 2024— Jeffrey Hunt.

All rights reserved. This book or any portion thereof may not be reproduced or used in any manner whatsoever without the expresss written permission of the publisher except for the use of brief quotations in a book review.

https://www.artofjeffreyhunt.com

CONTENTS:

WITCHES

MONSTERS

GHOSTS

PUMPKINS

SCARY PLACES

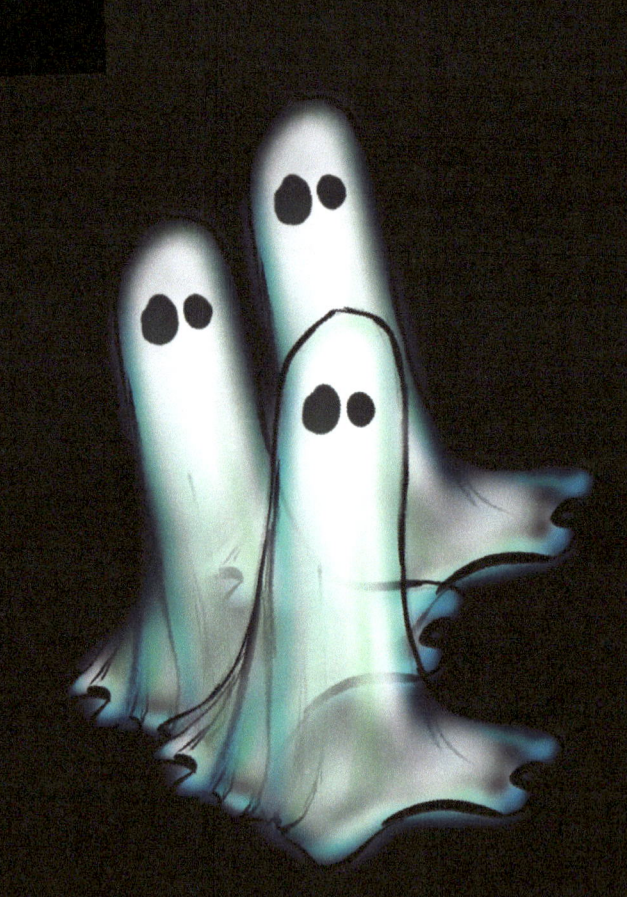

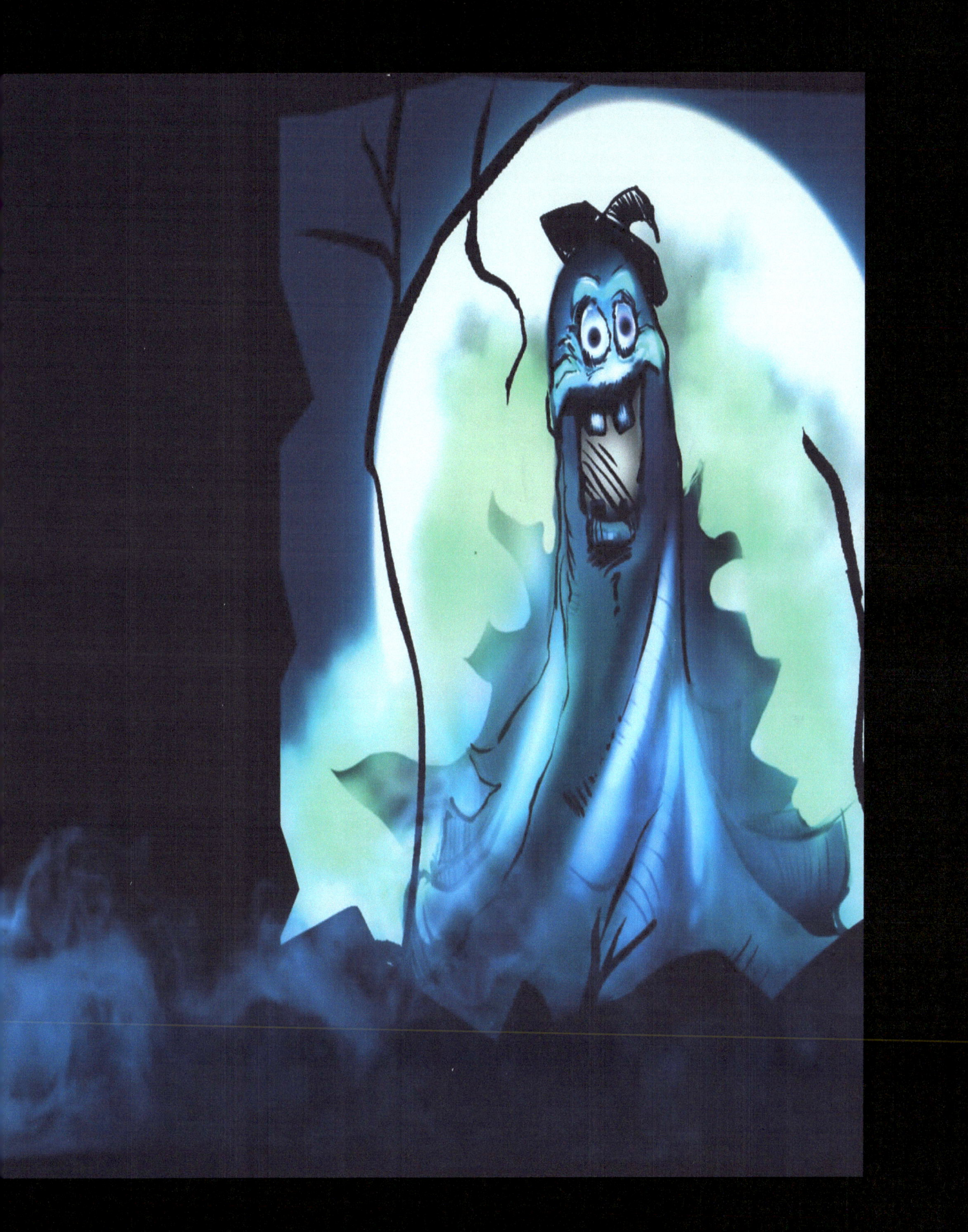

WITCHES

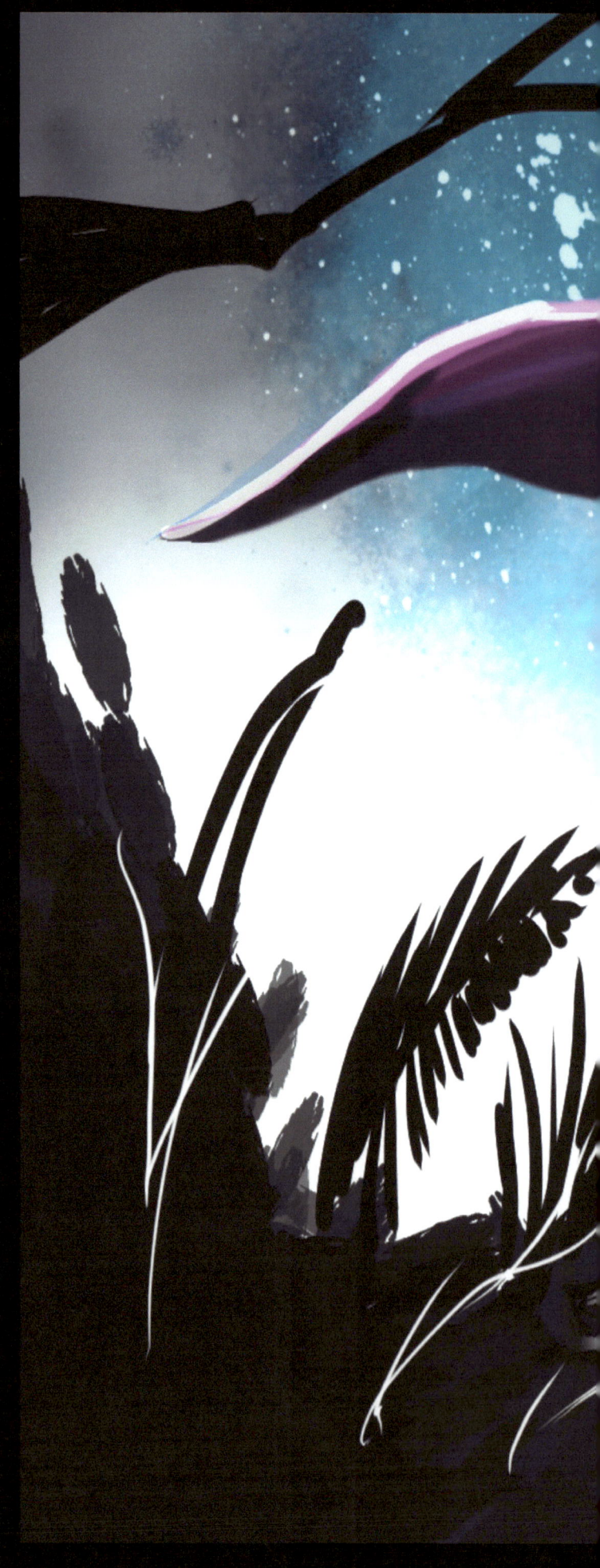

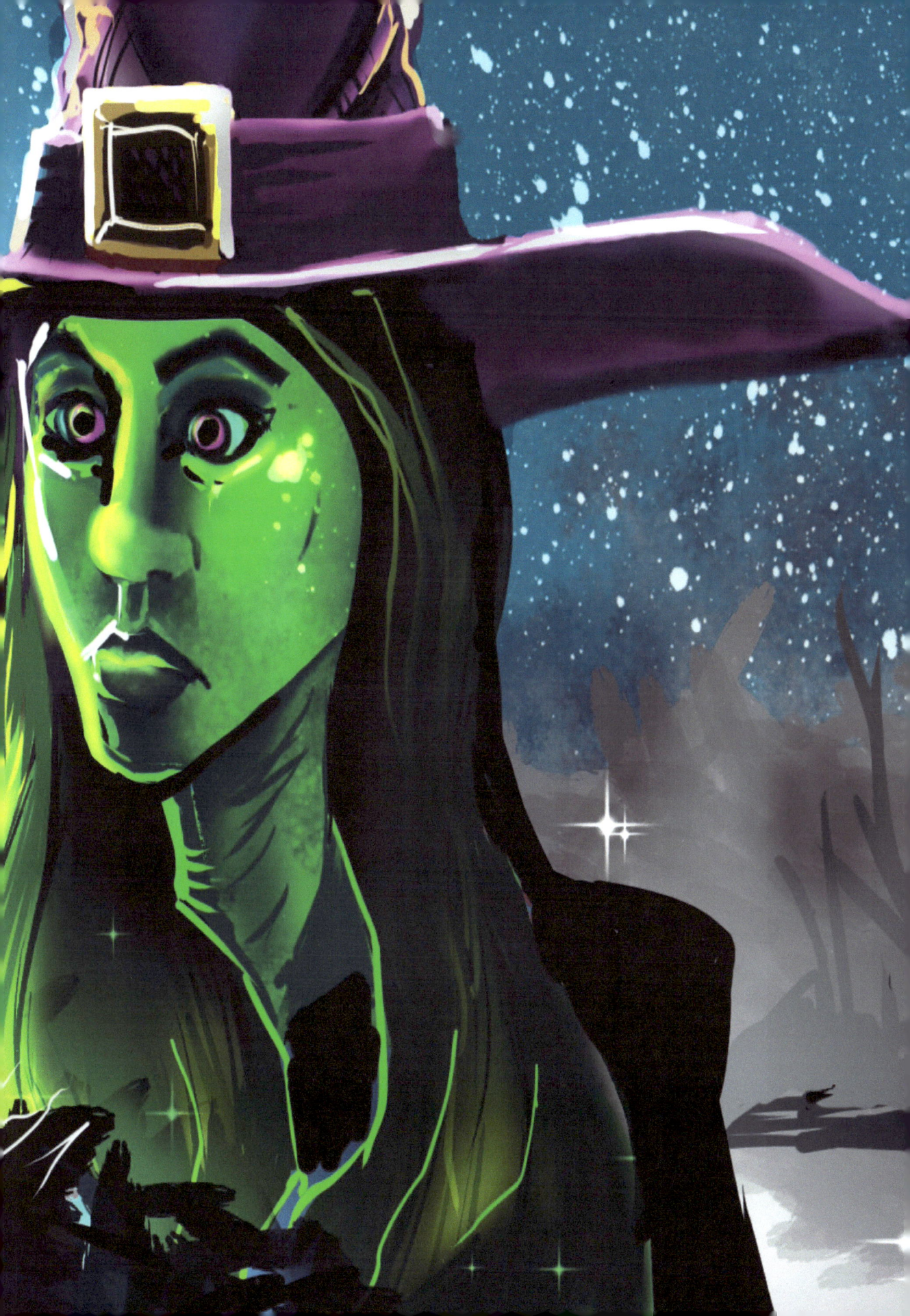

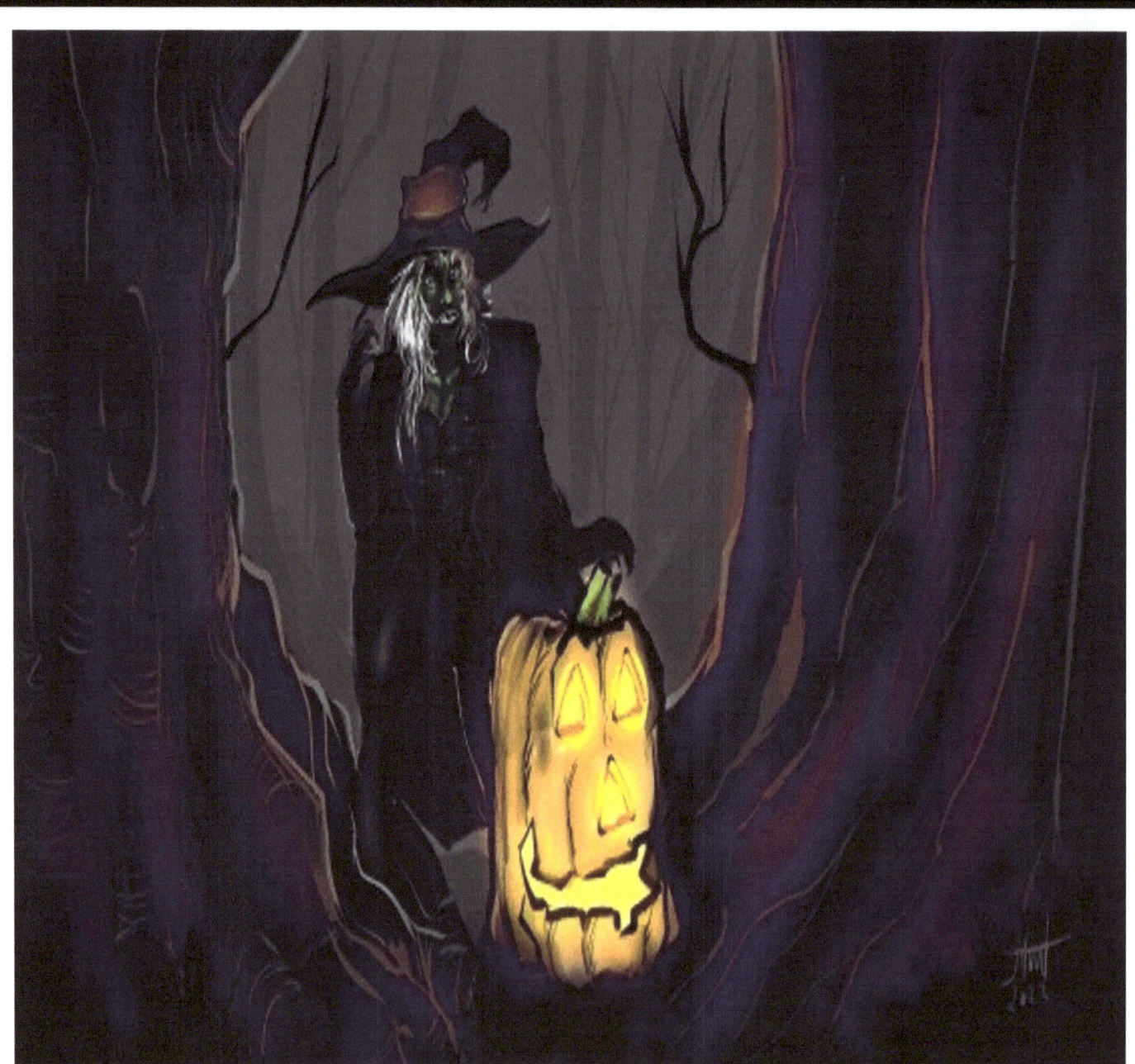

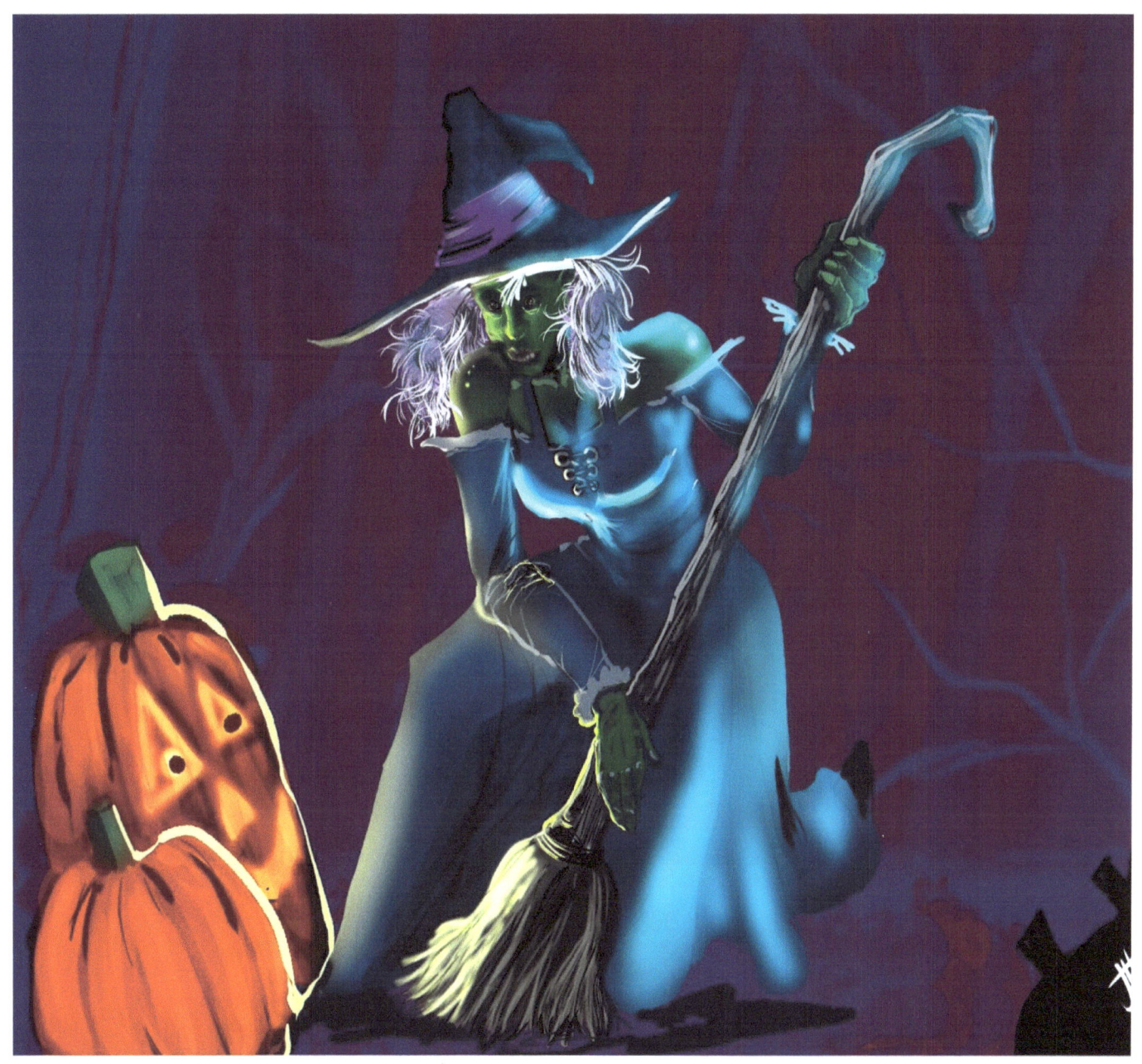

SWEEPING AWAY THE NIGHT

MONSTERS

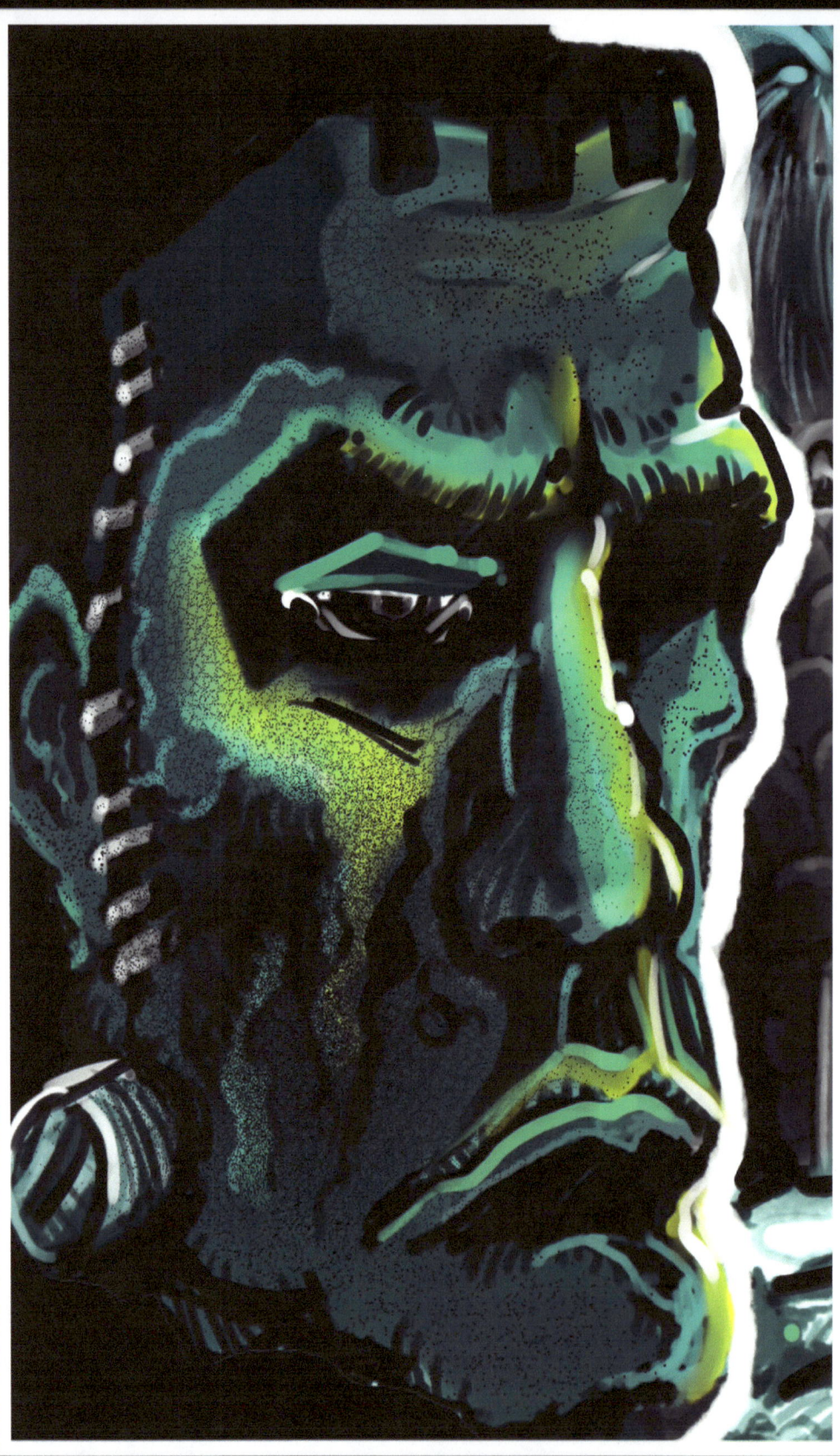

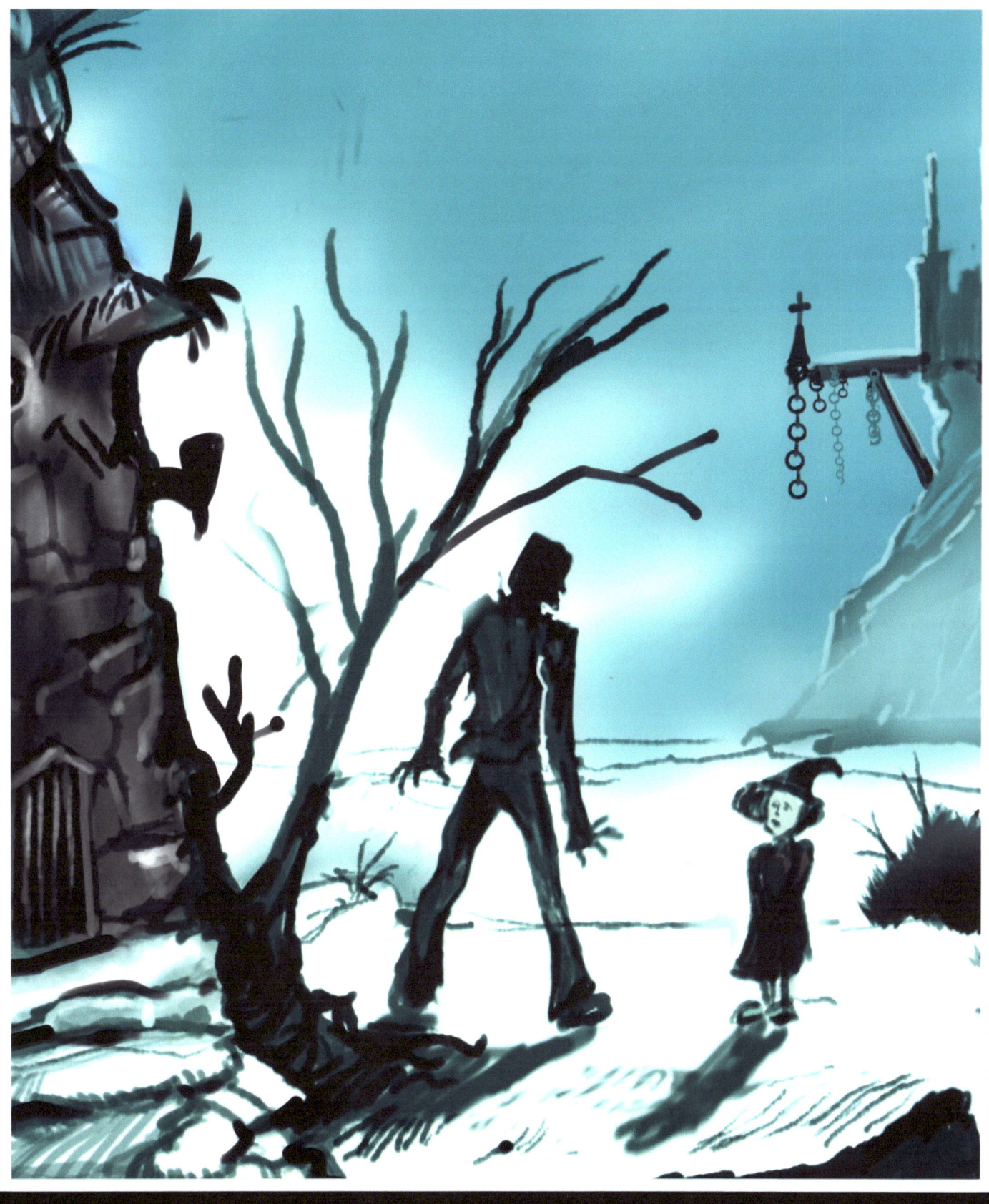

THE MONSTER MEETS THE GIRL

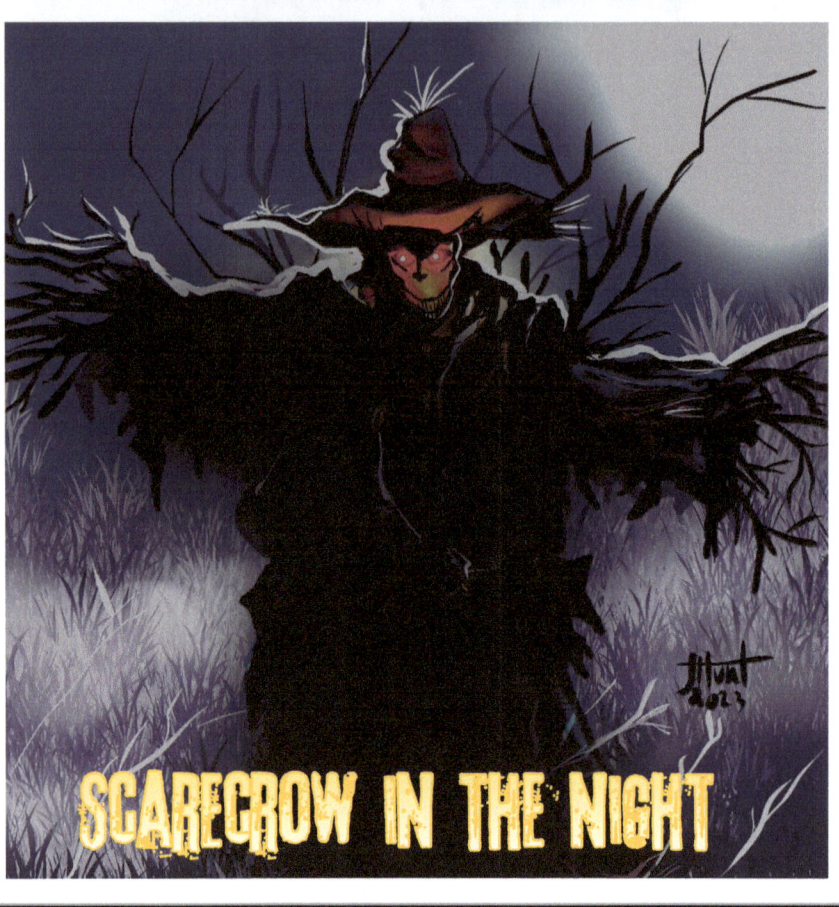
SCARECROW IN THE NIGHT

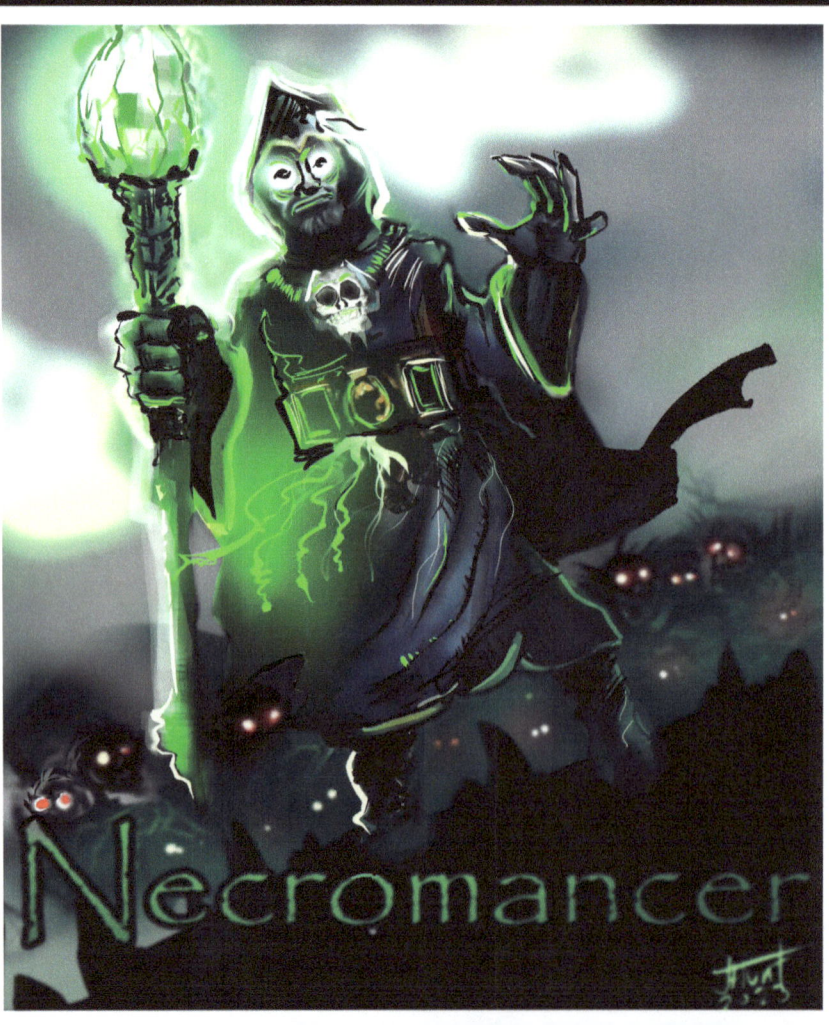
Necromancer

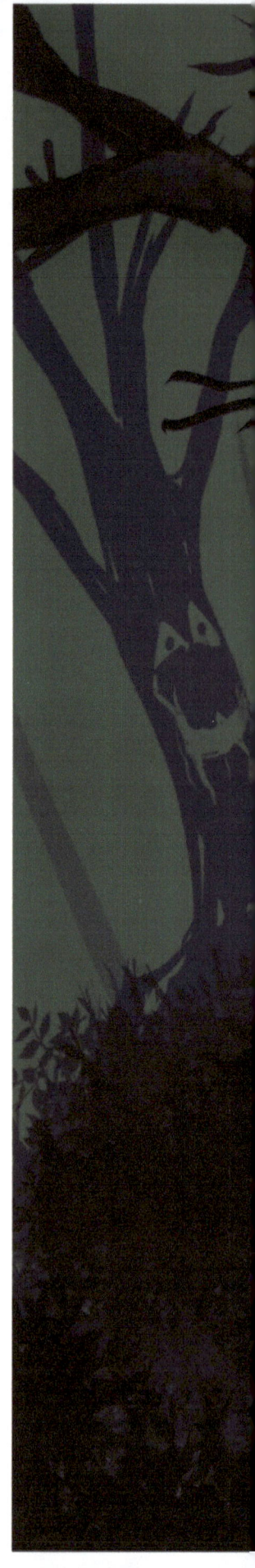

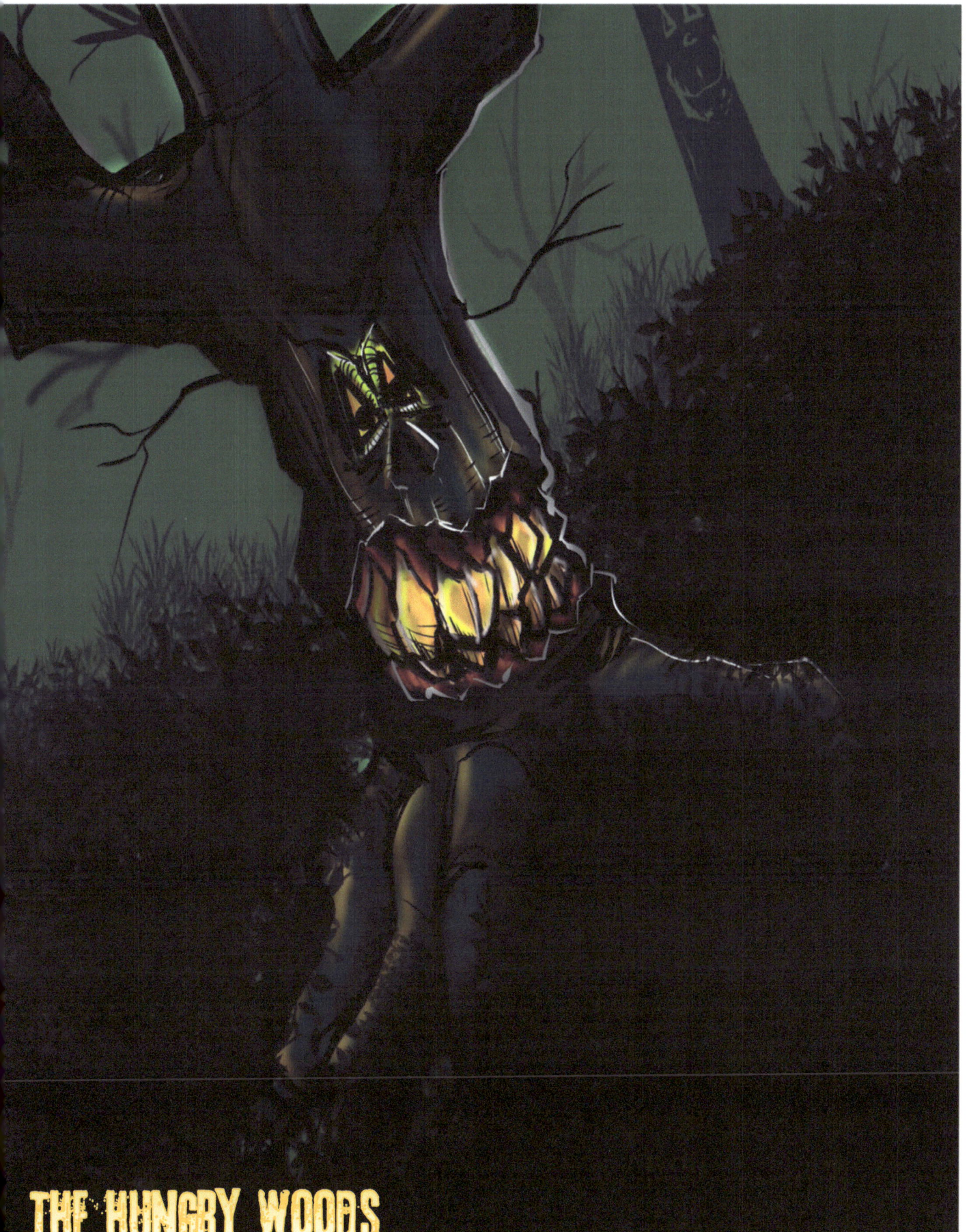

THE HUNGRY WOODS

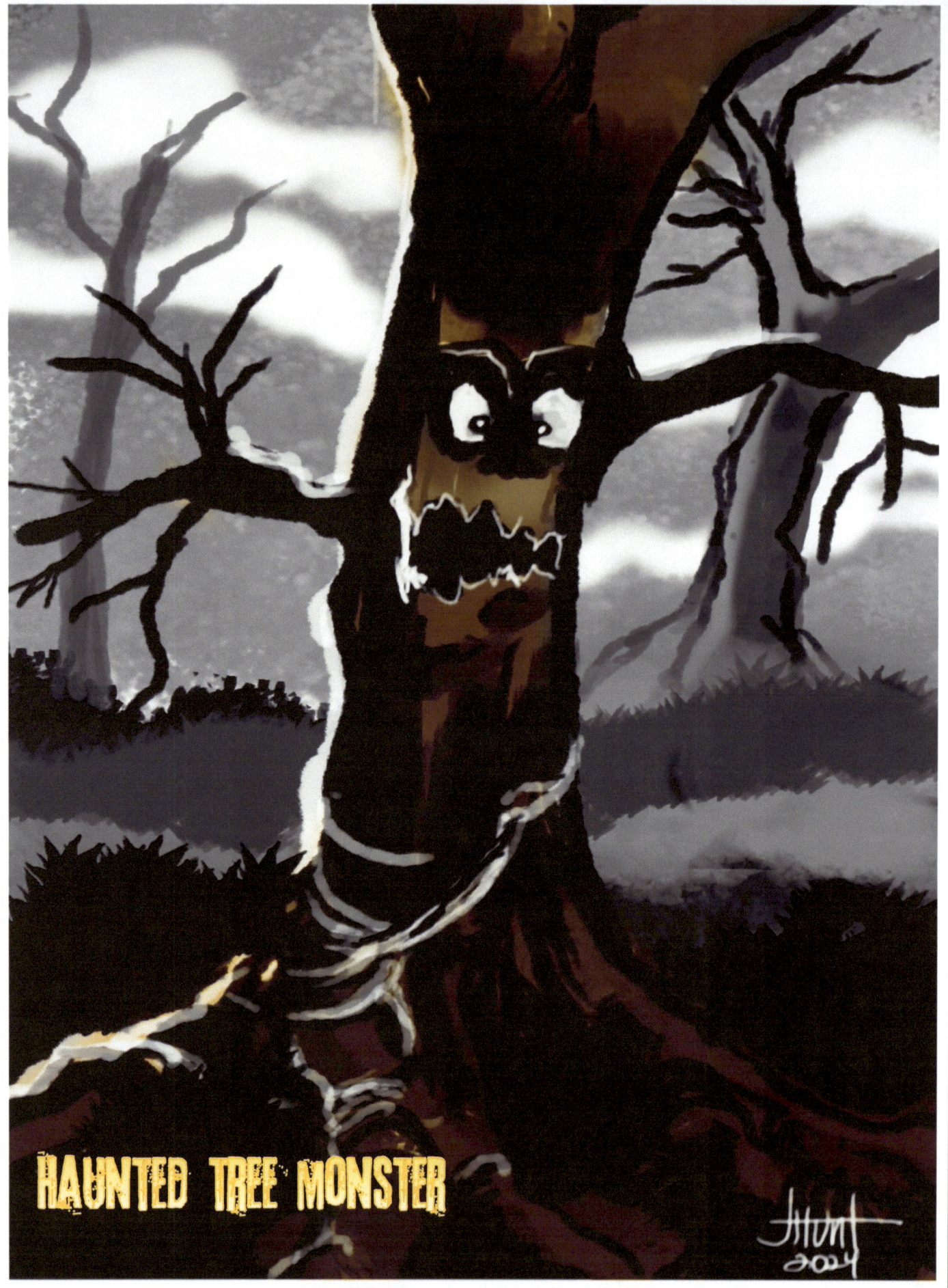

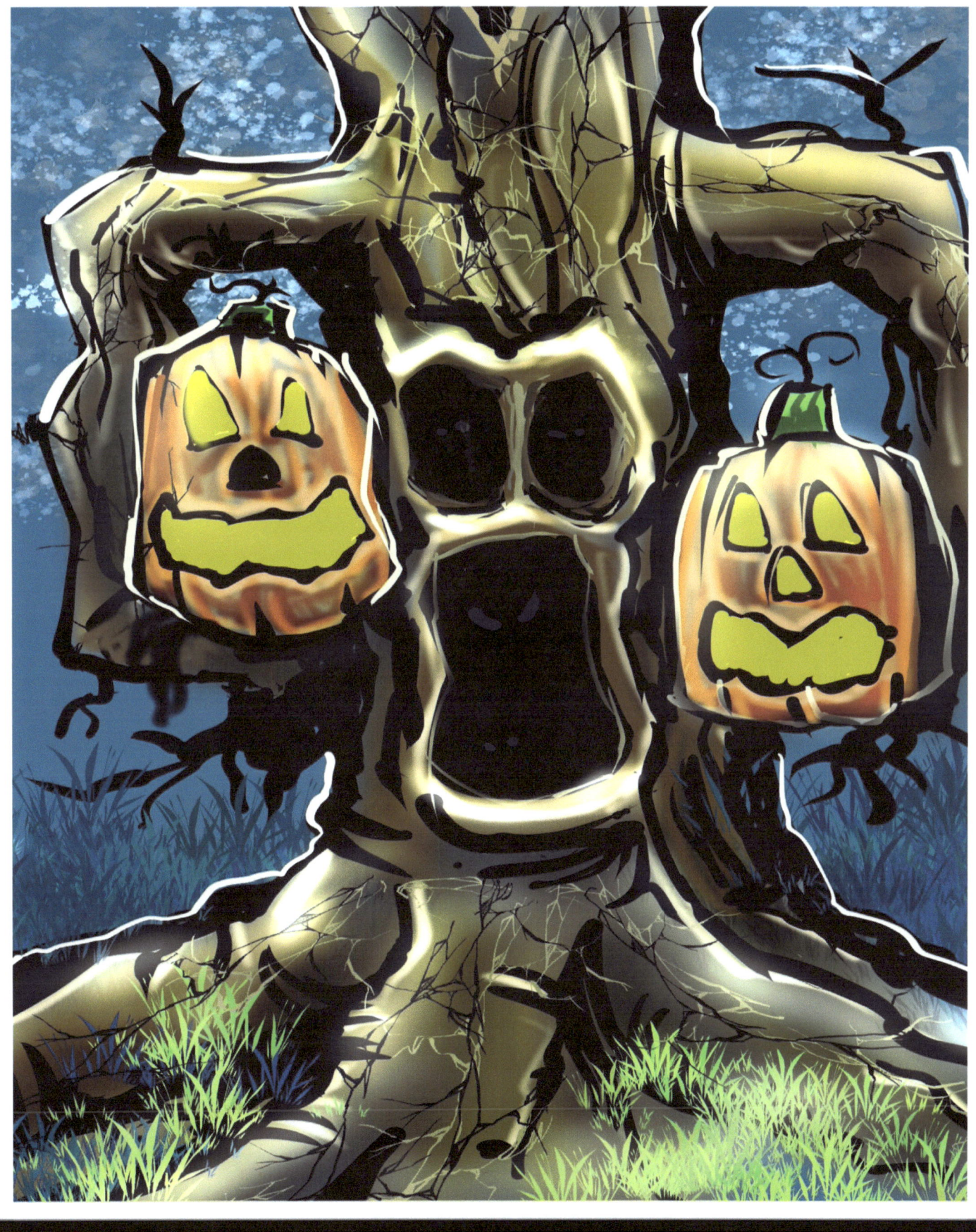
THE PUMPKIN TREE

SCARY PLACES

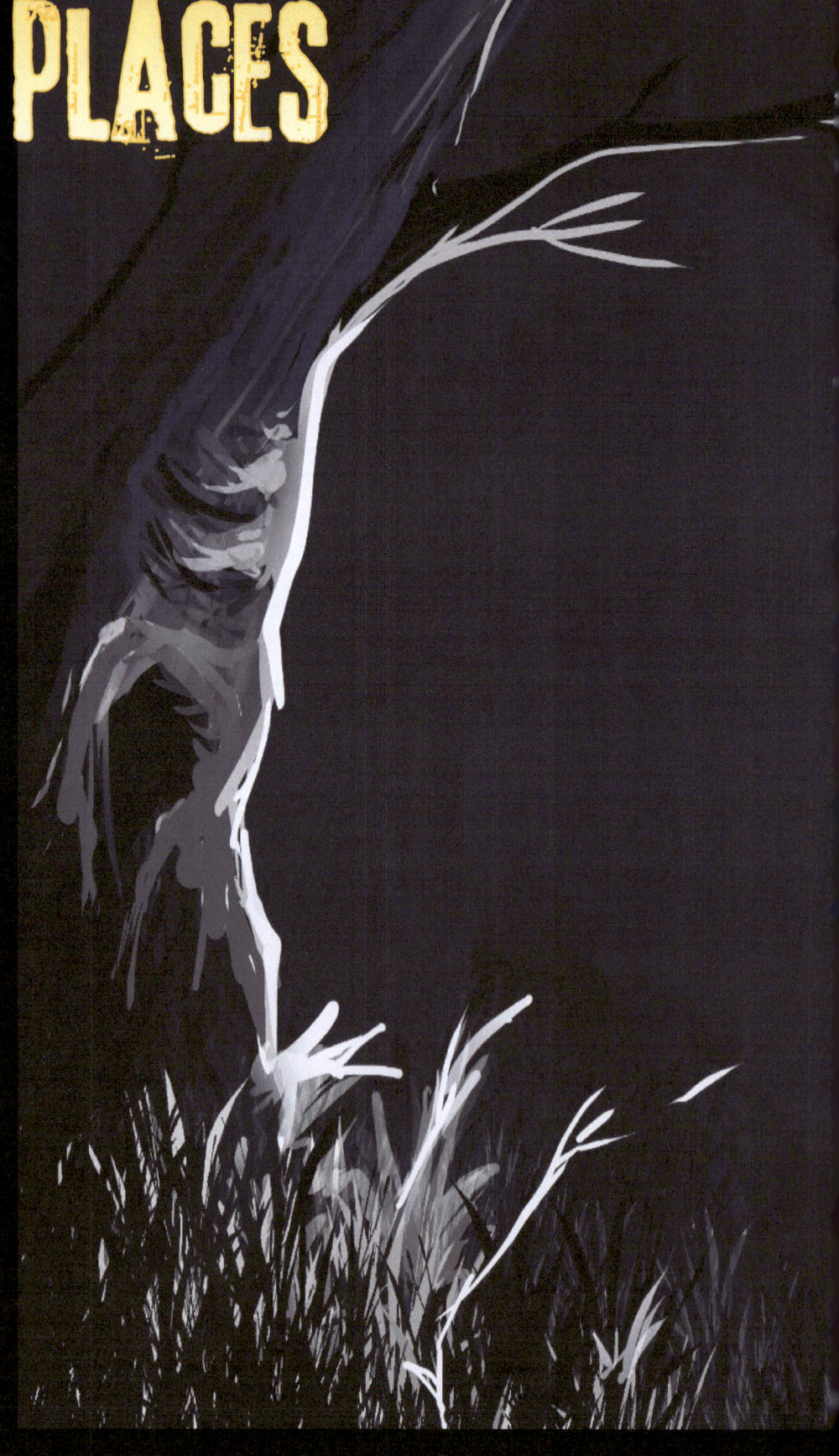

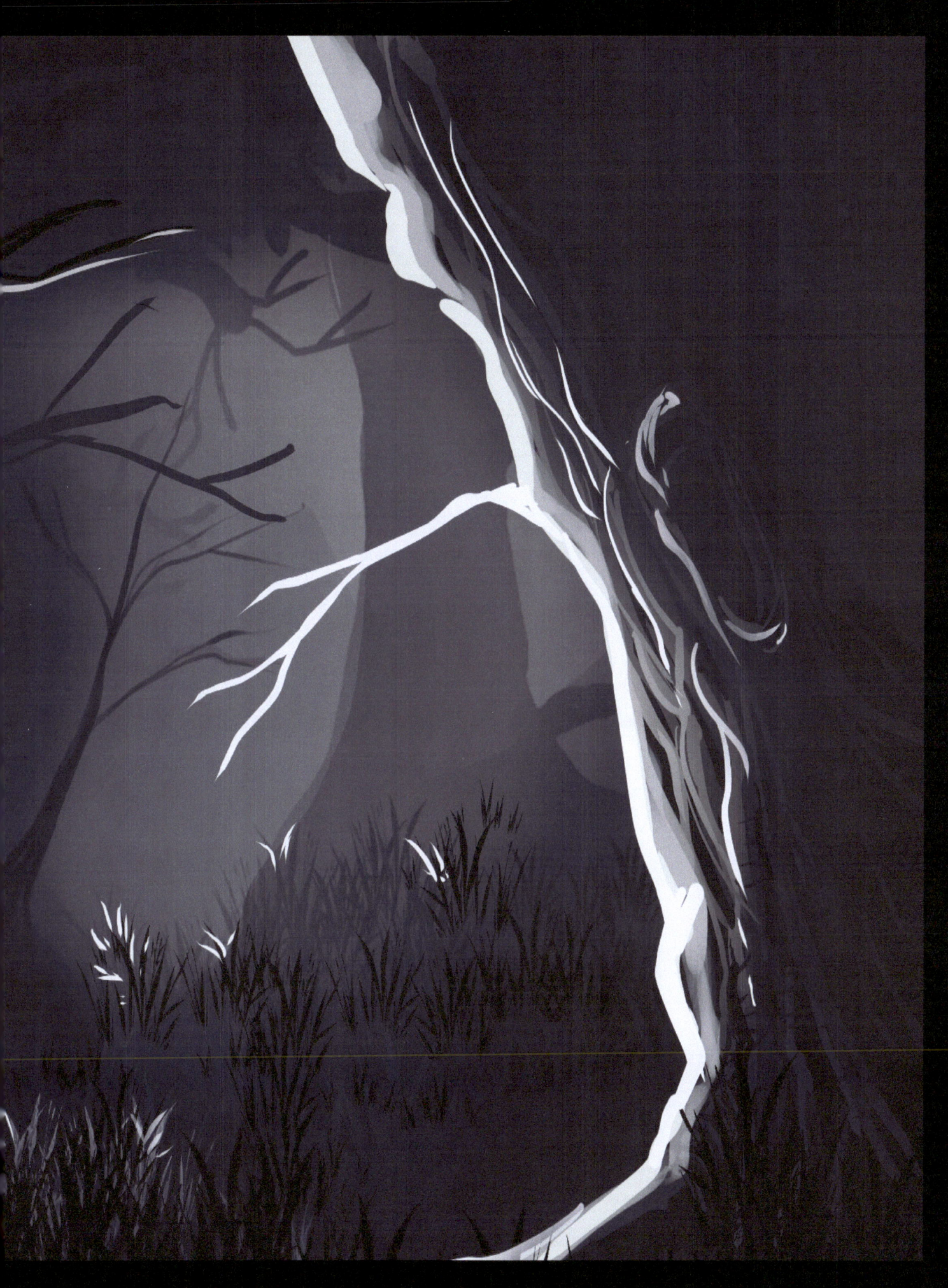

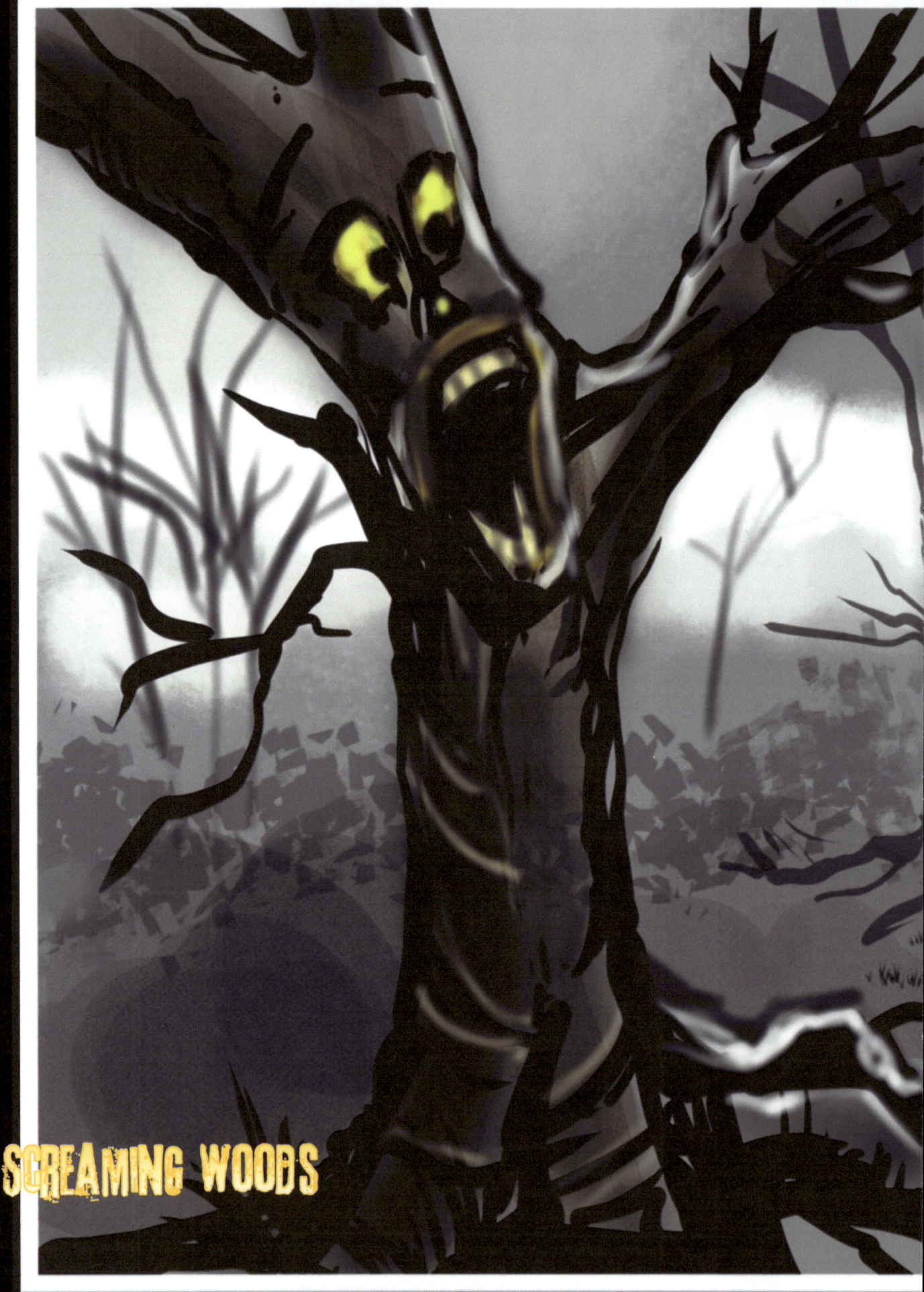

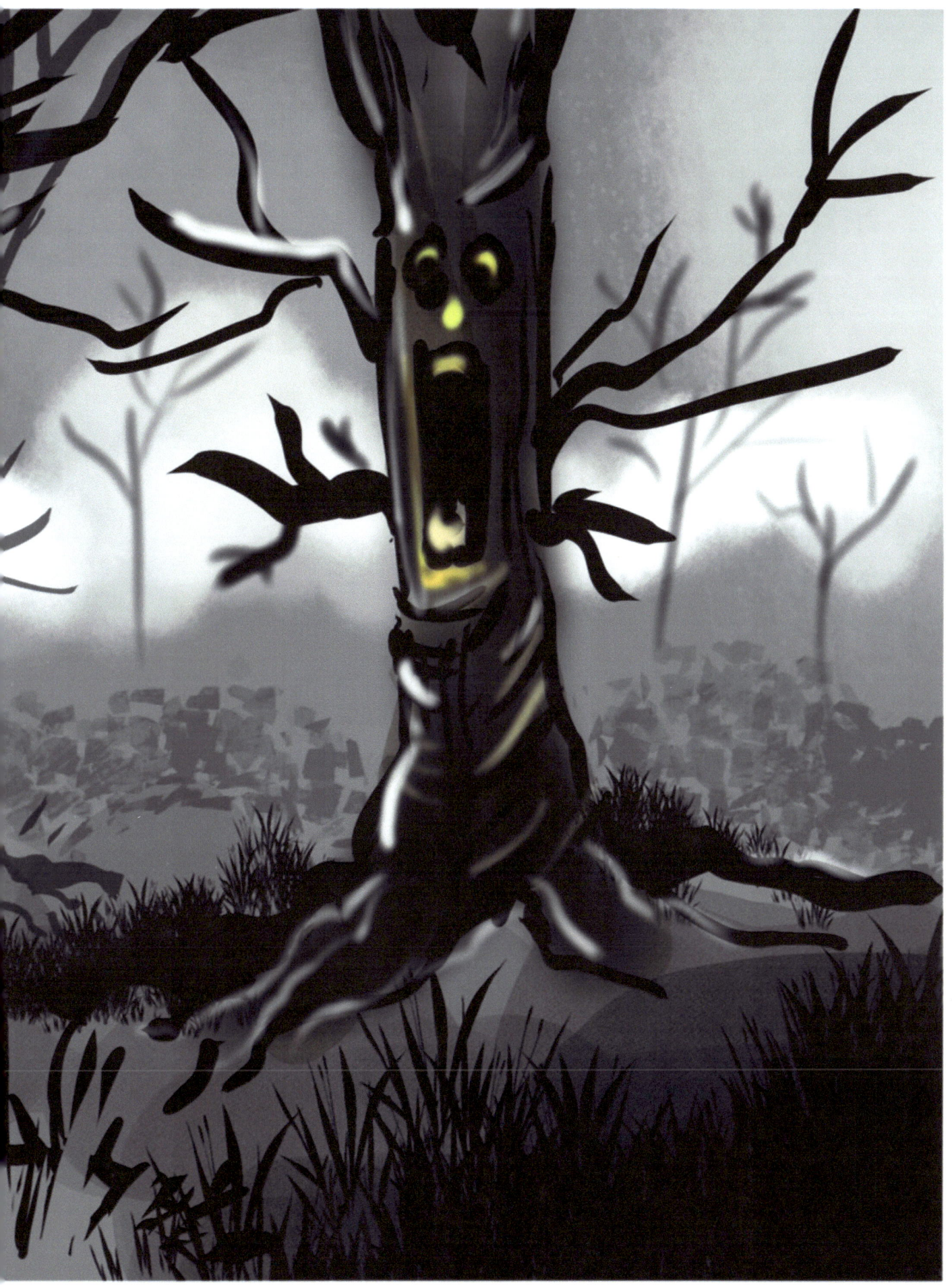

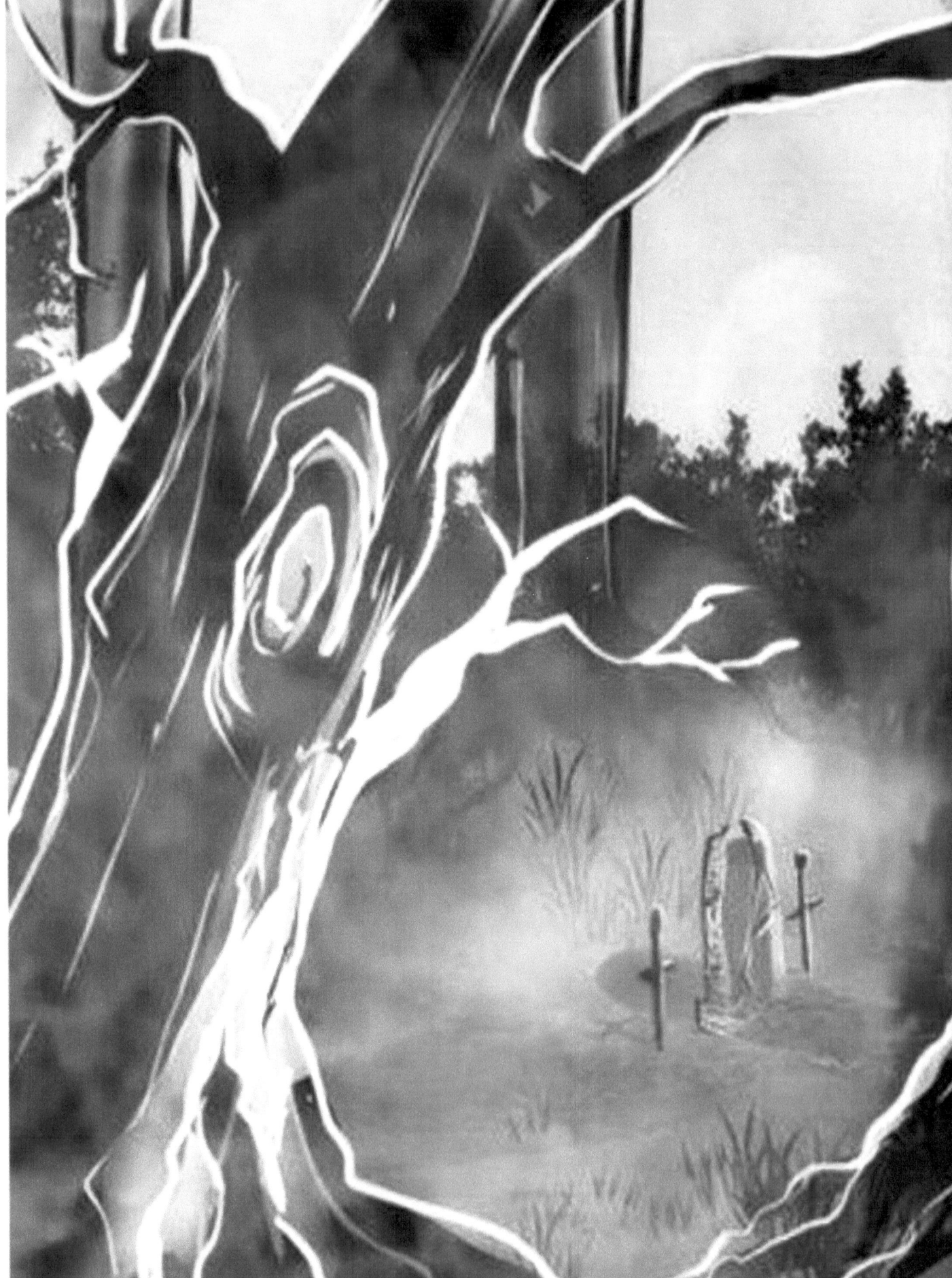

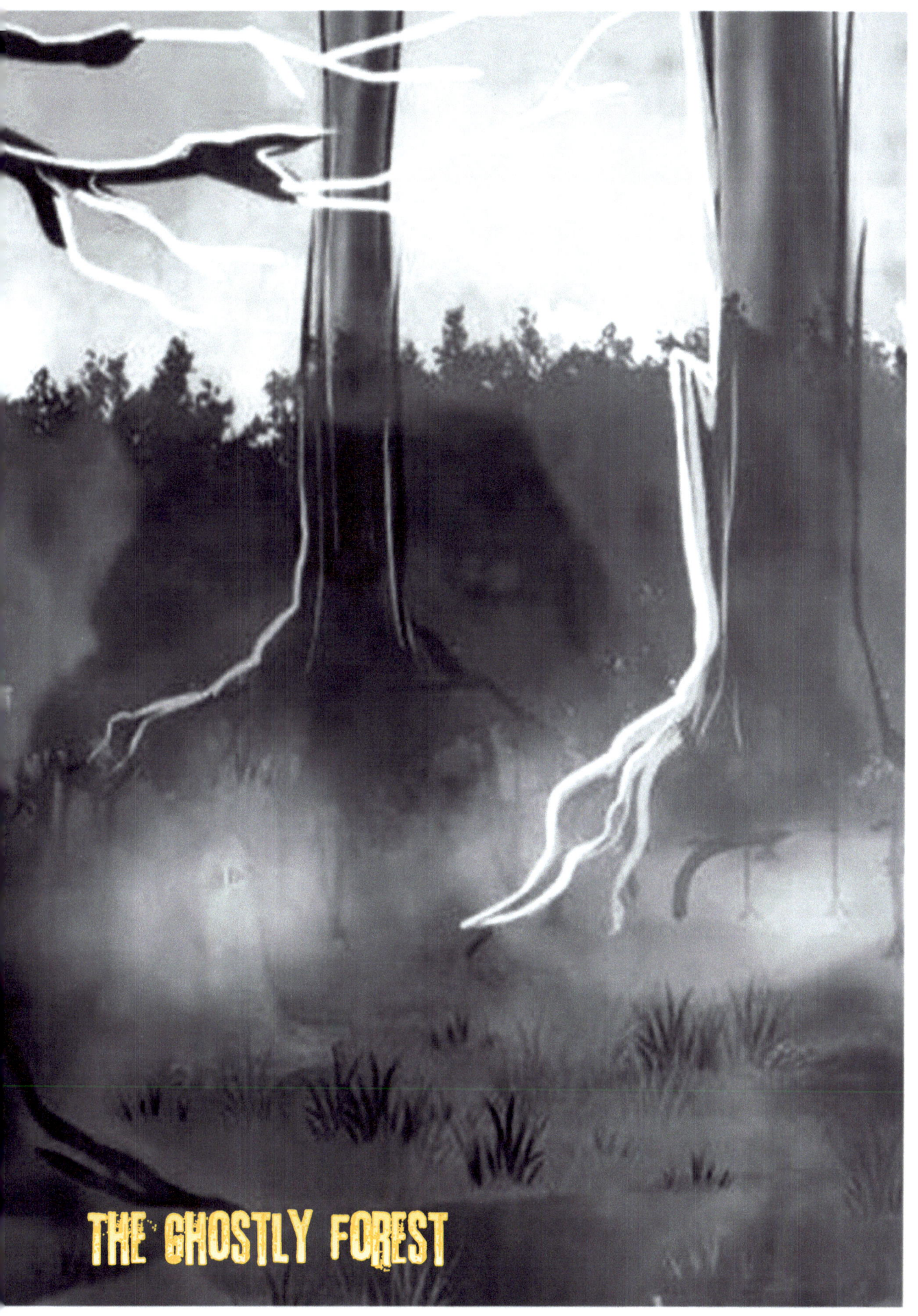

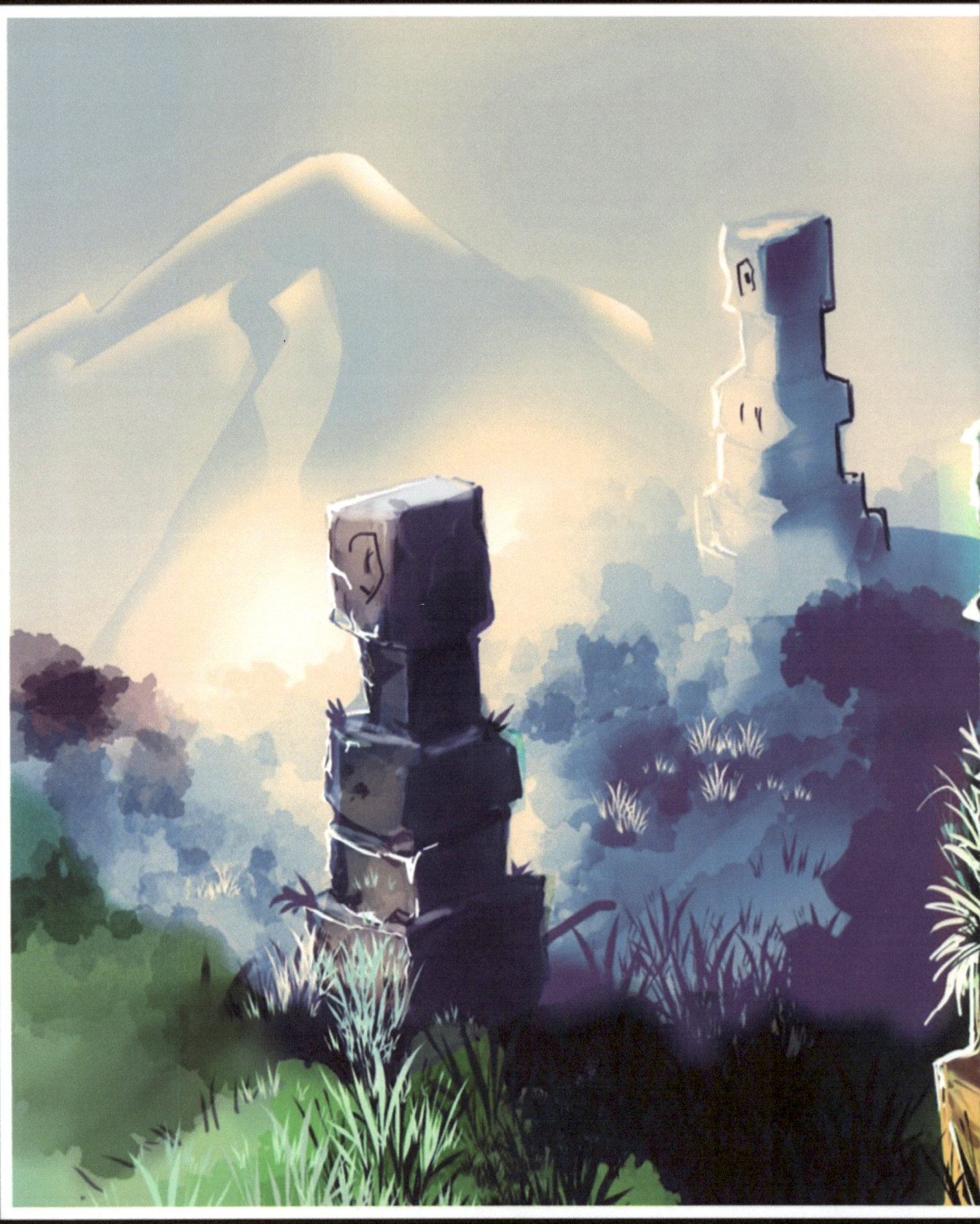

ANCIENT PILLARS OF TIME

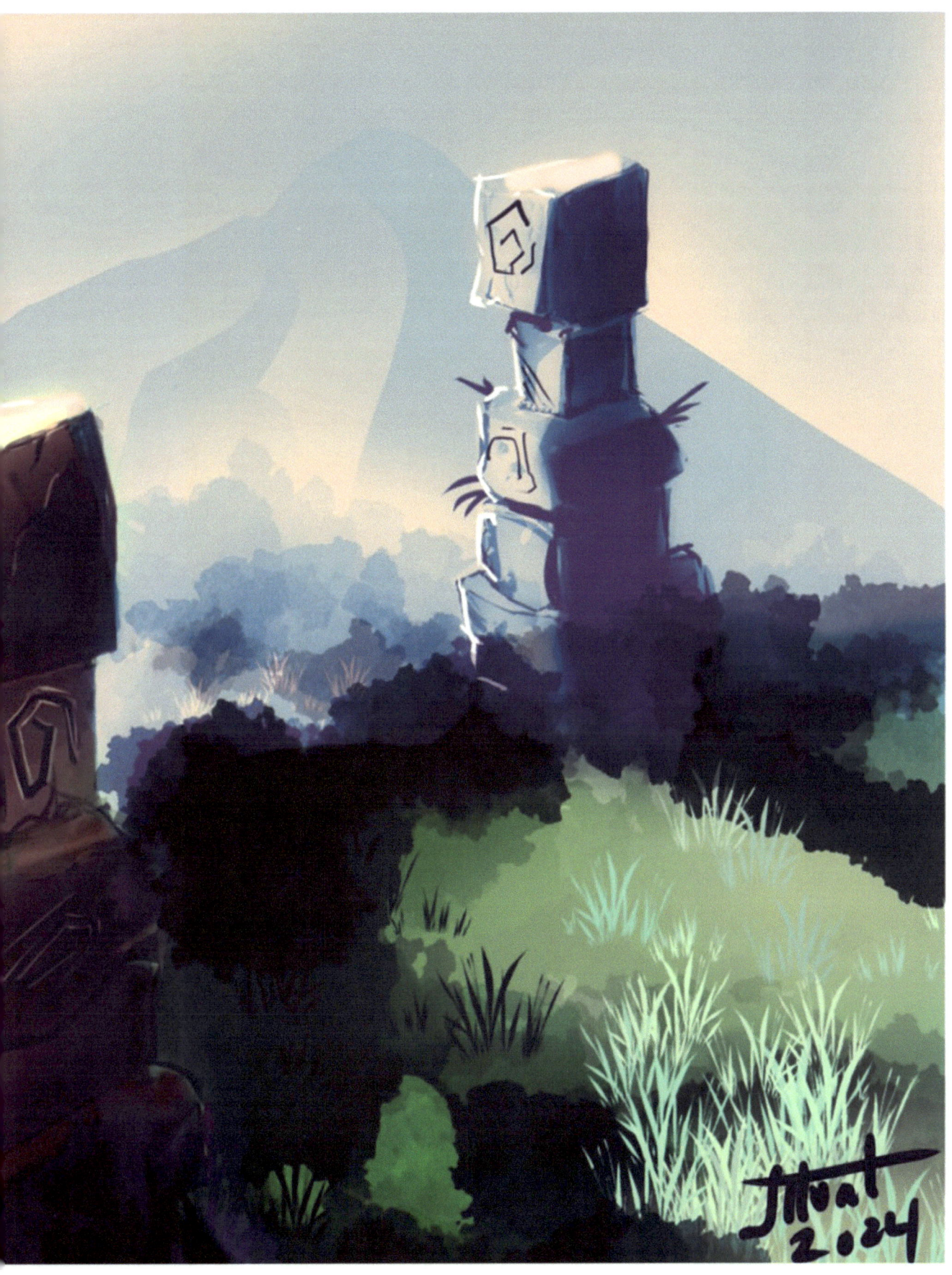

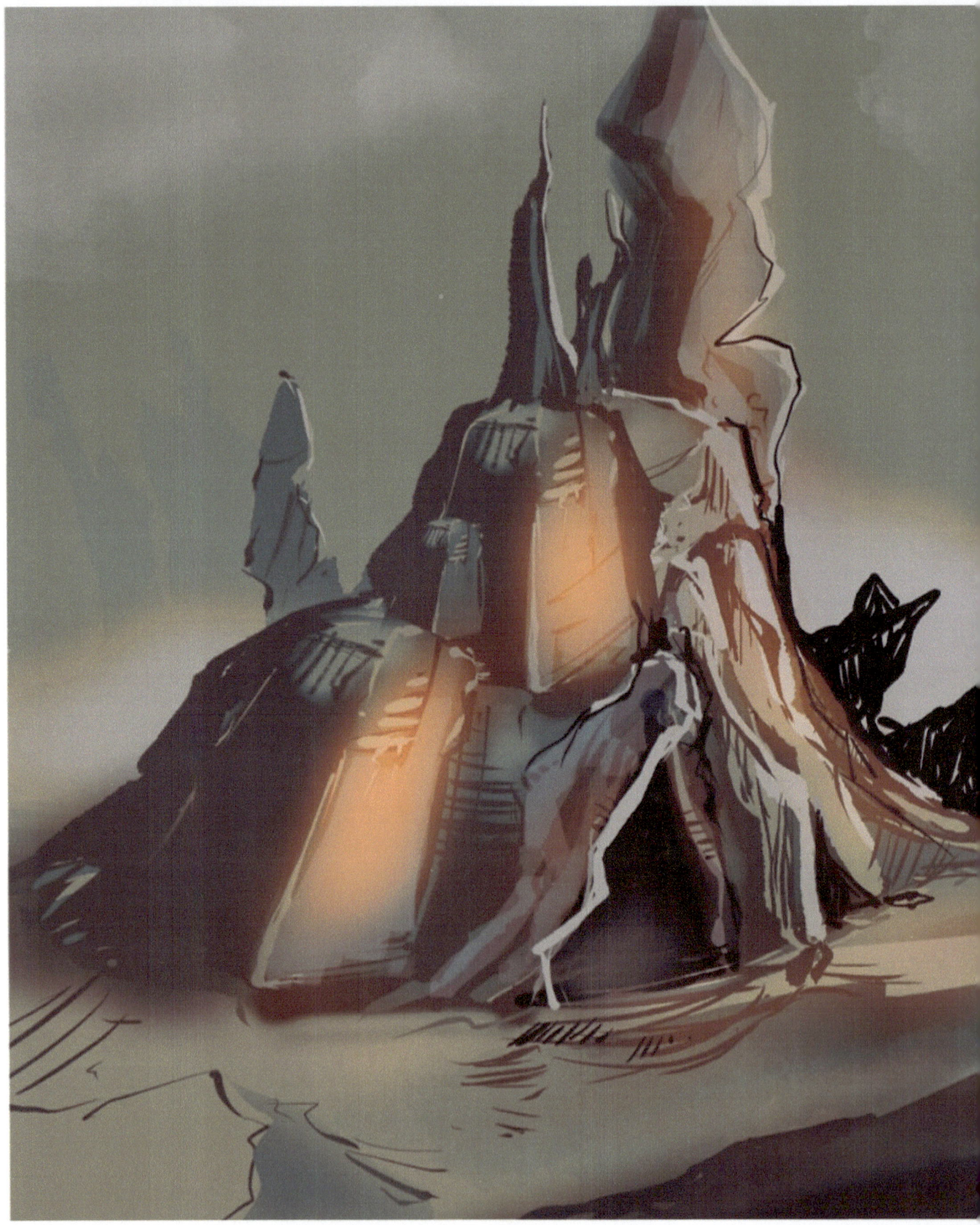

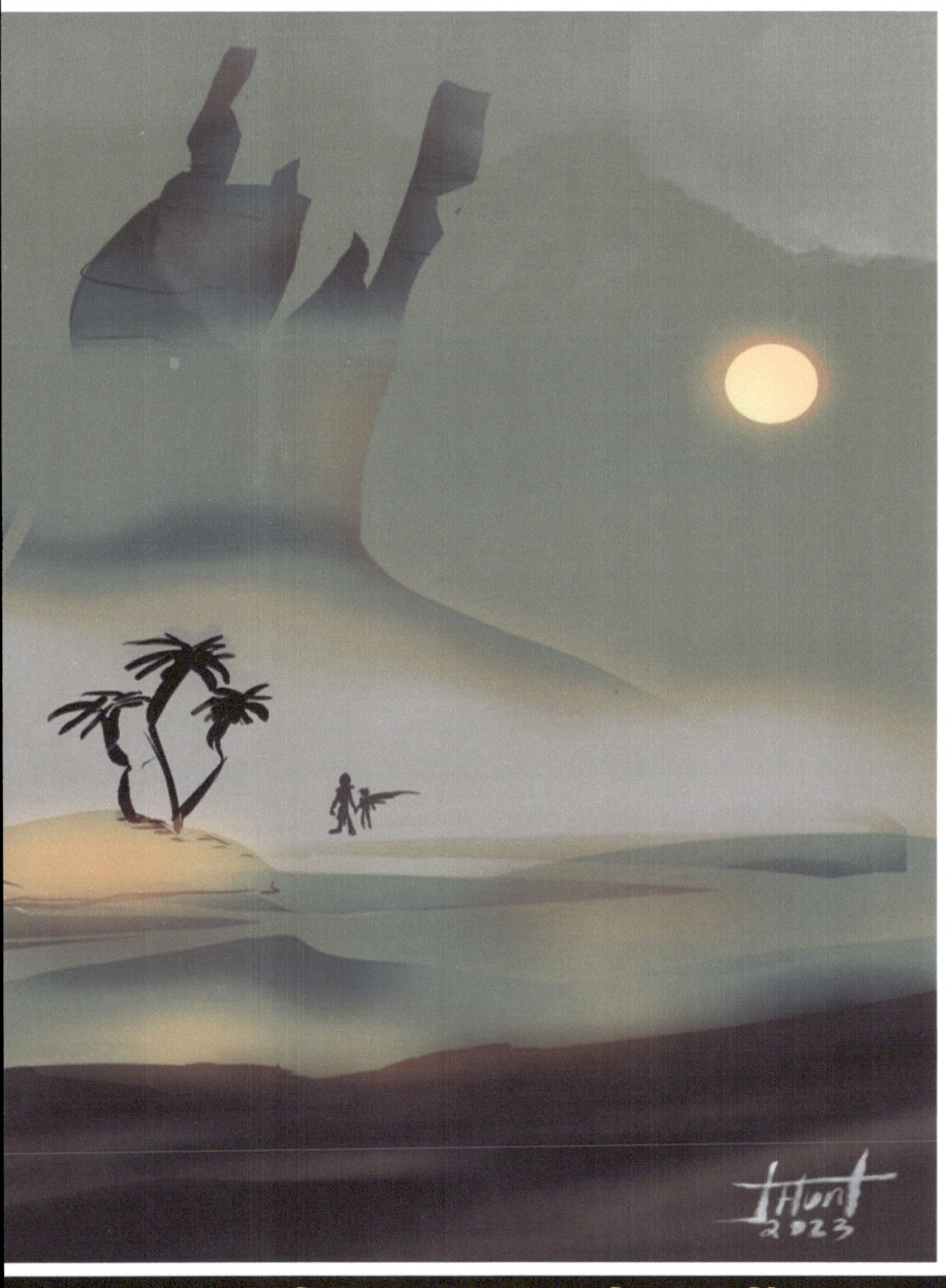

PUMPKINS

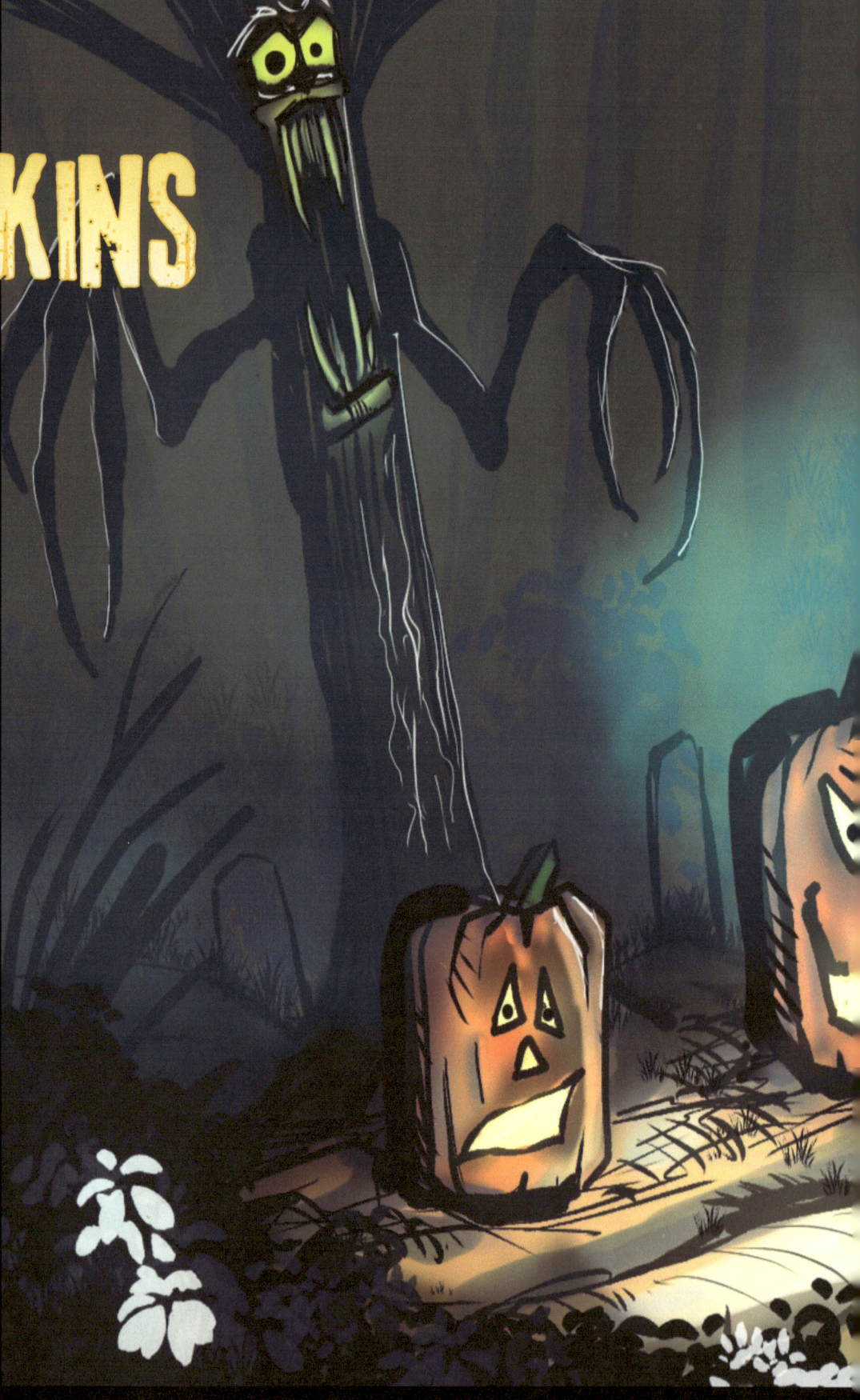

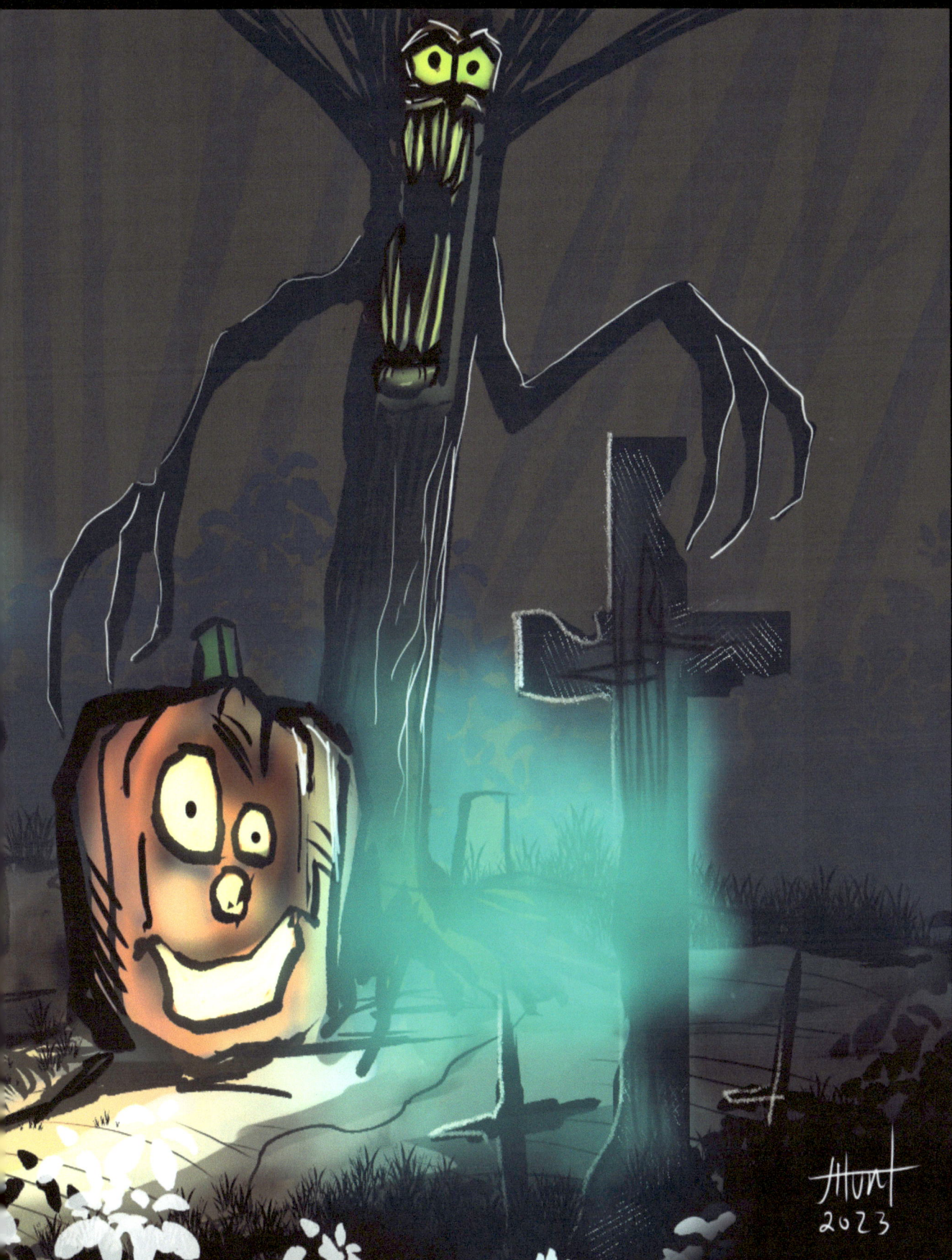

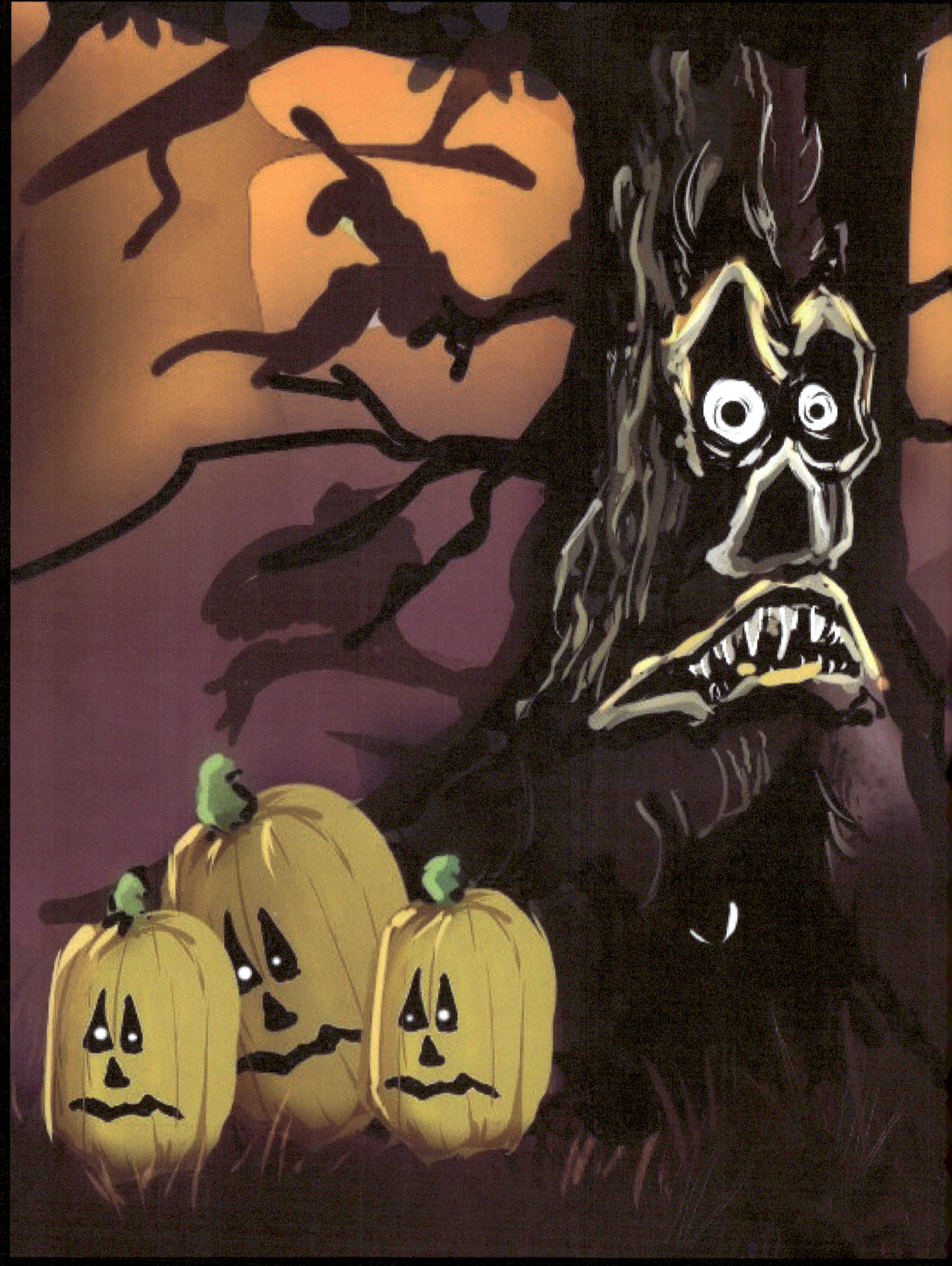

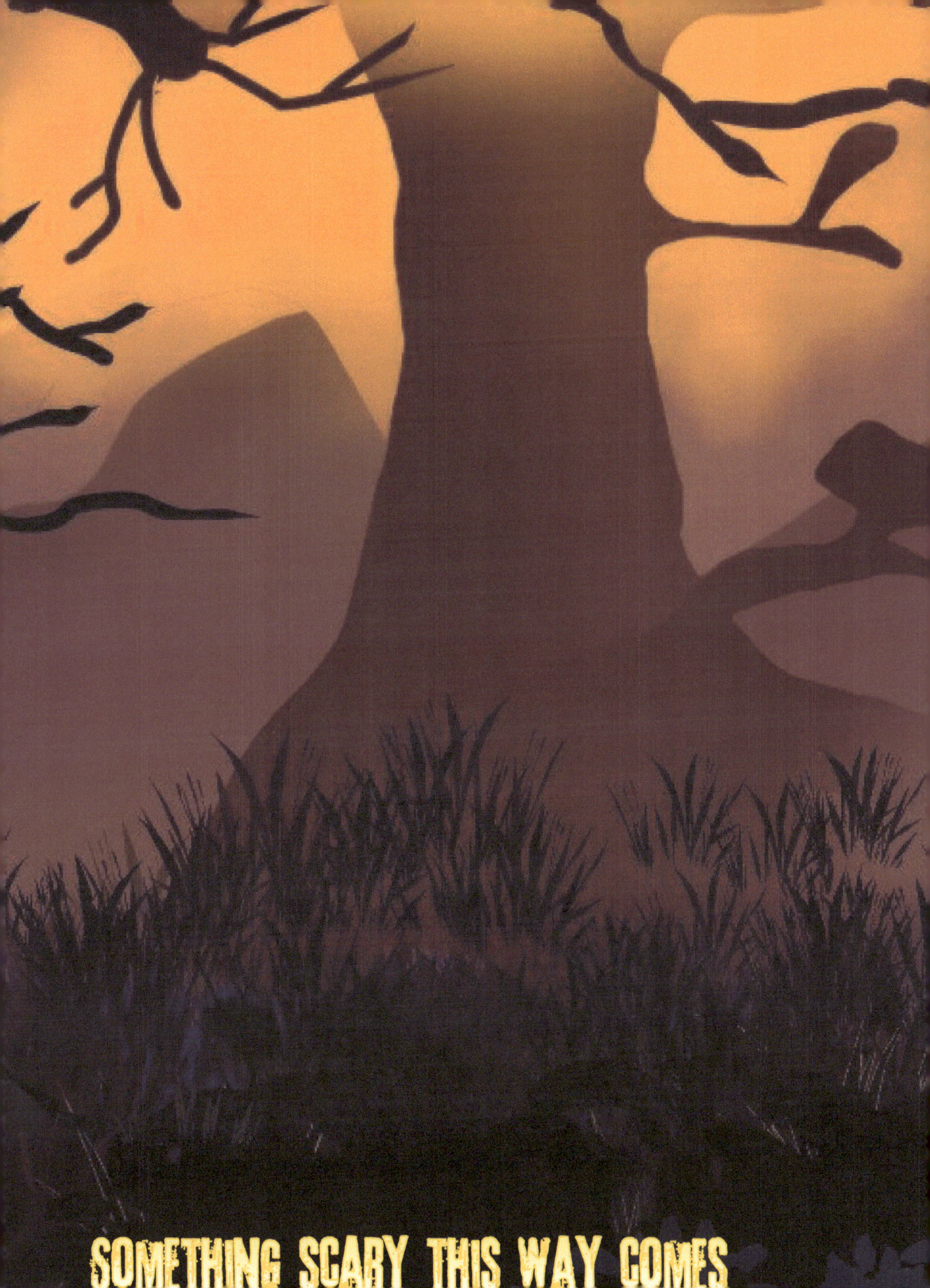

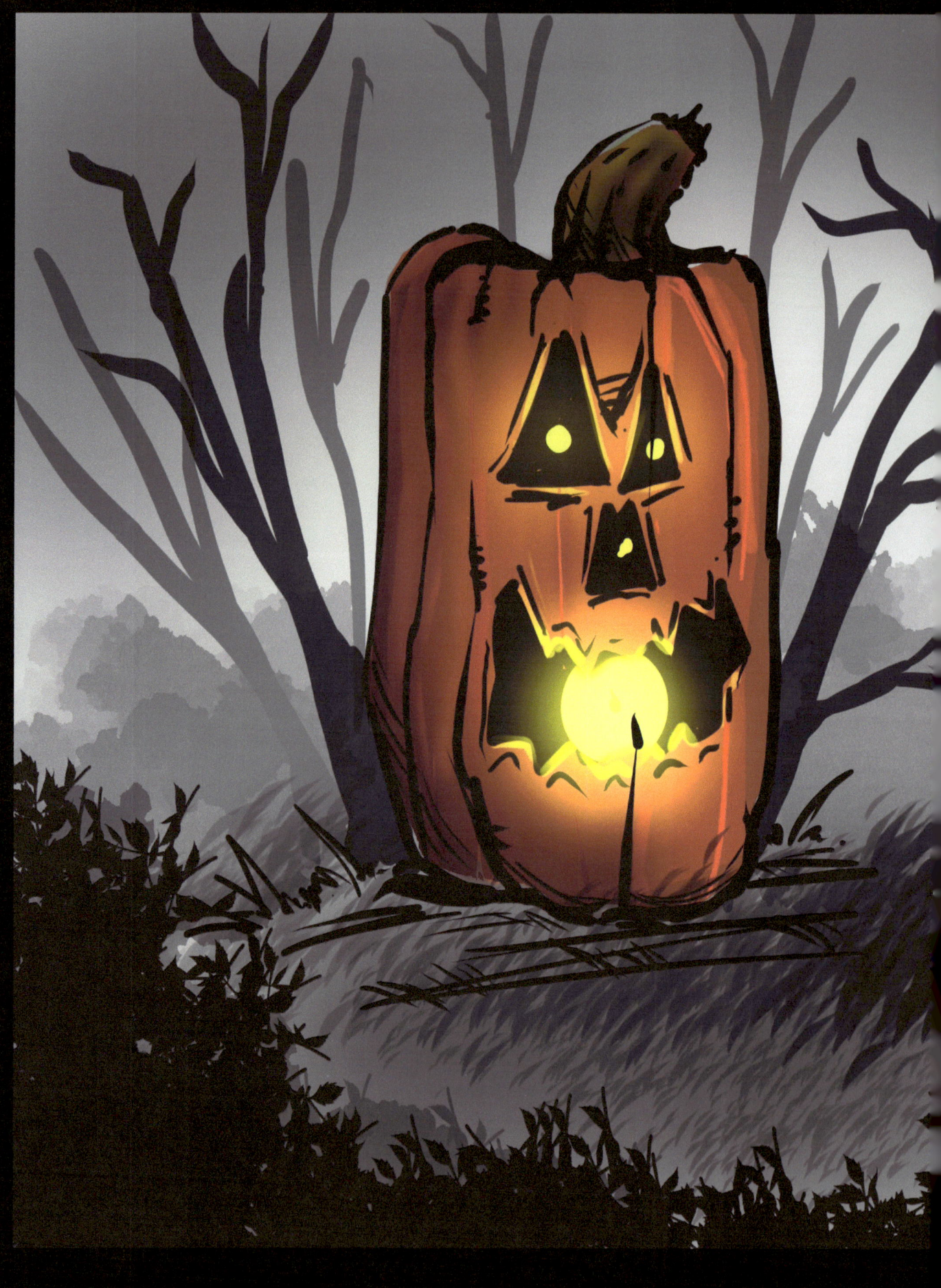

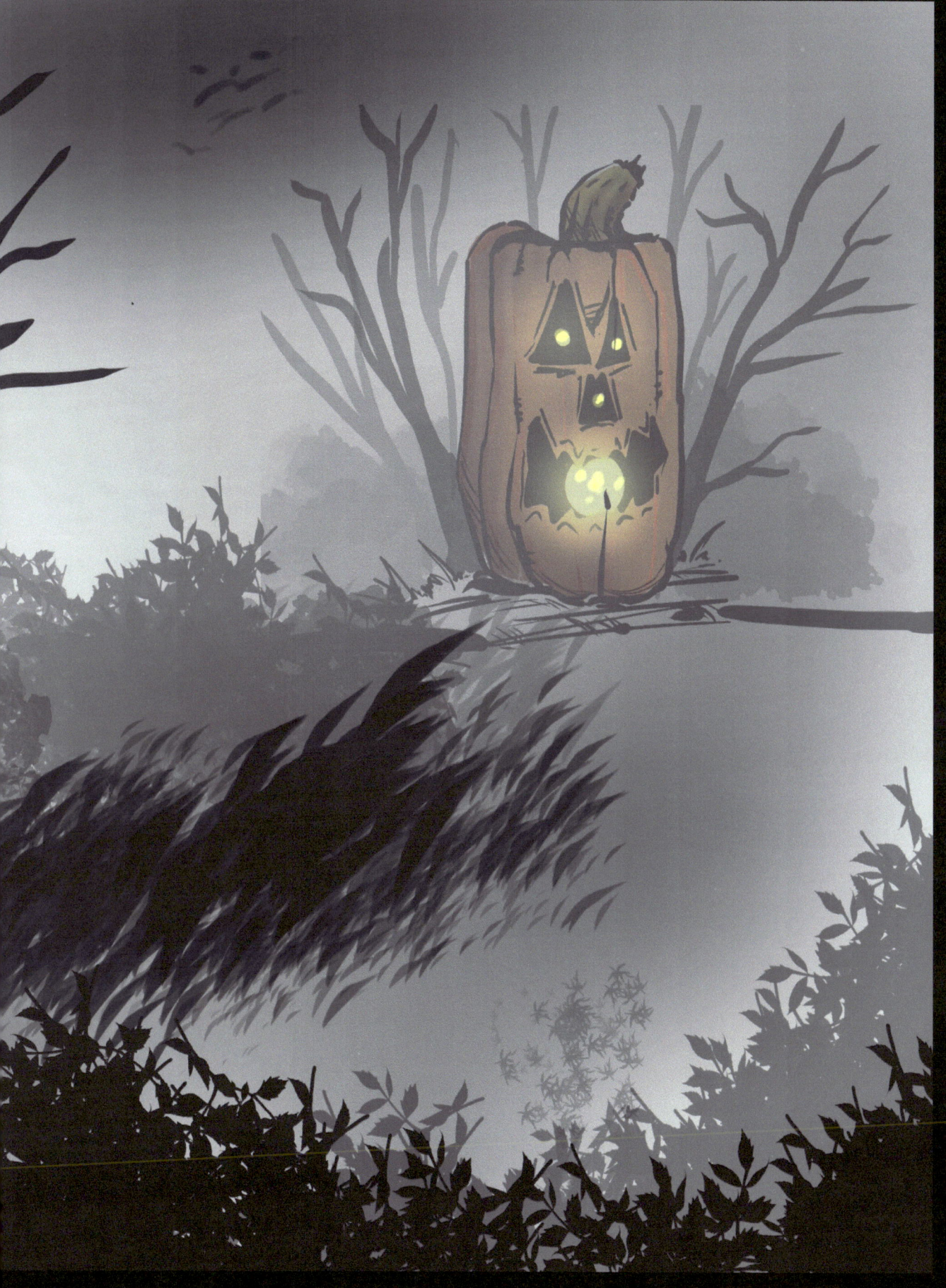

PUMPKIN BUSHES

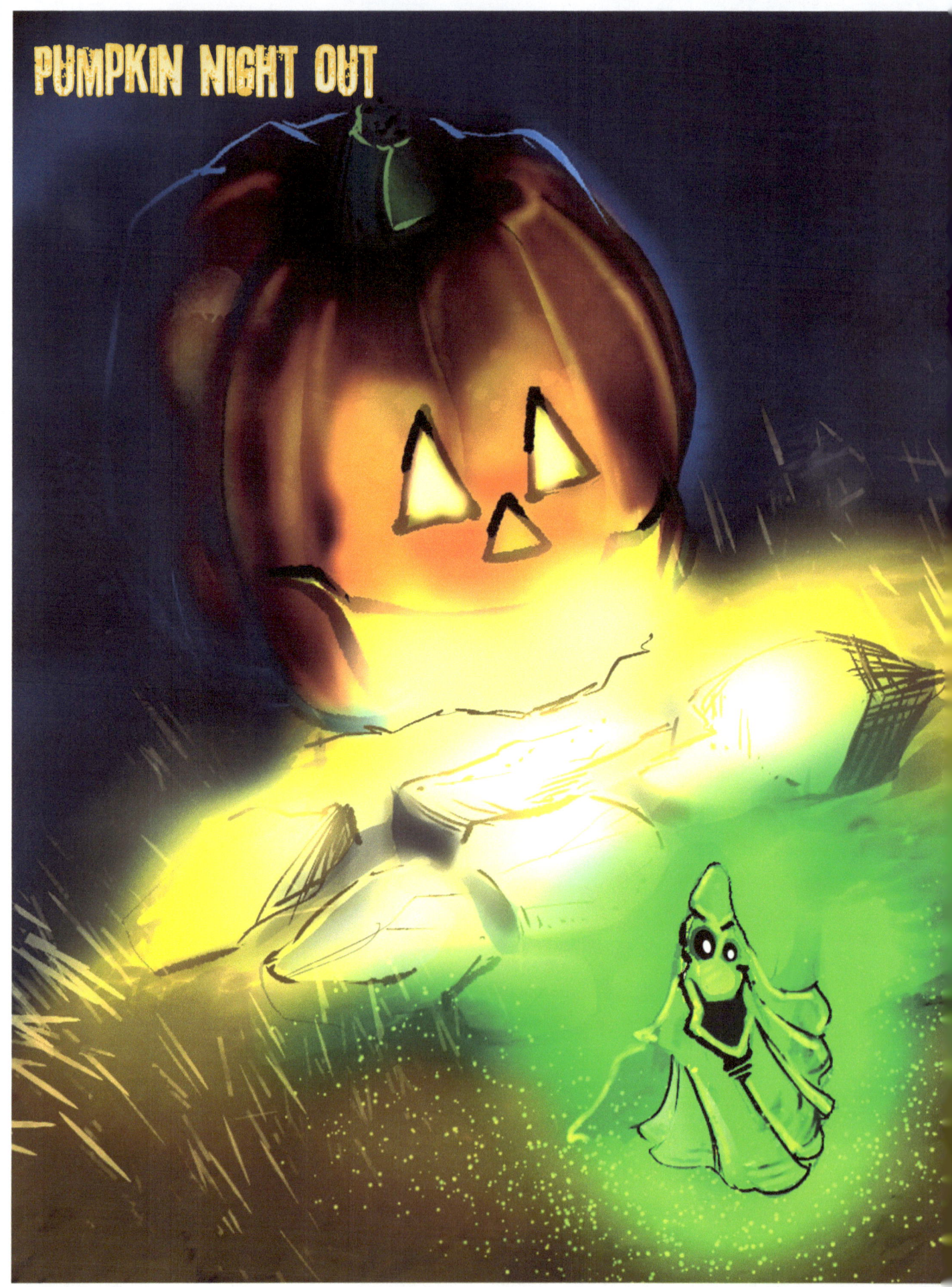

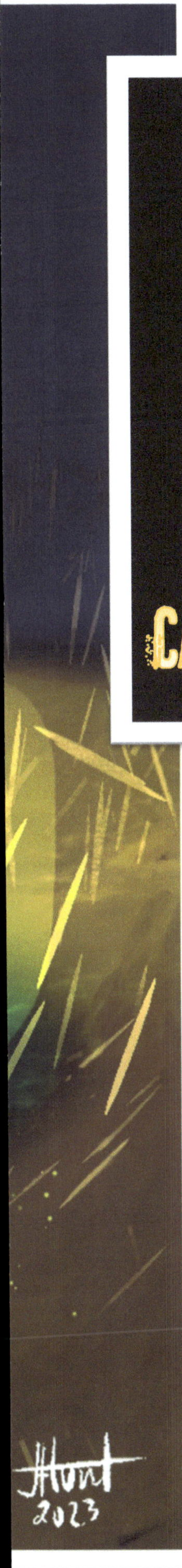

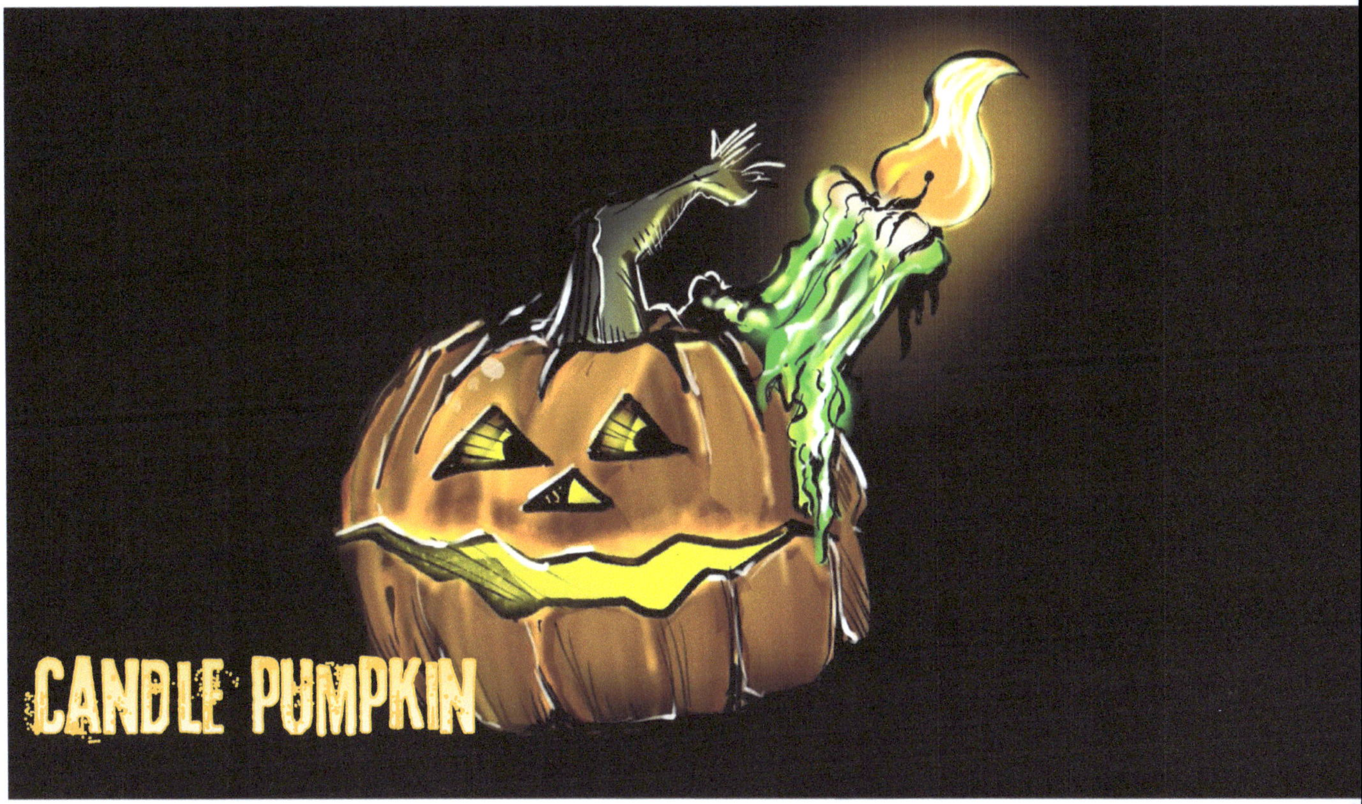

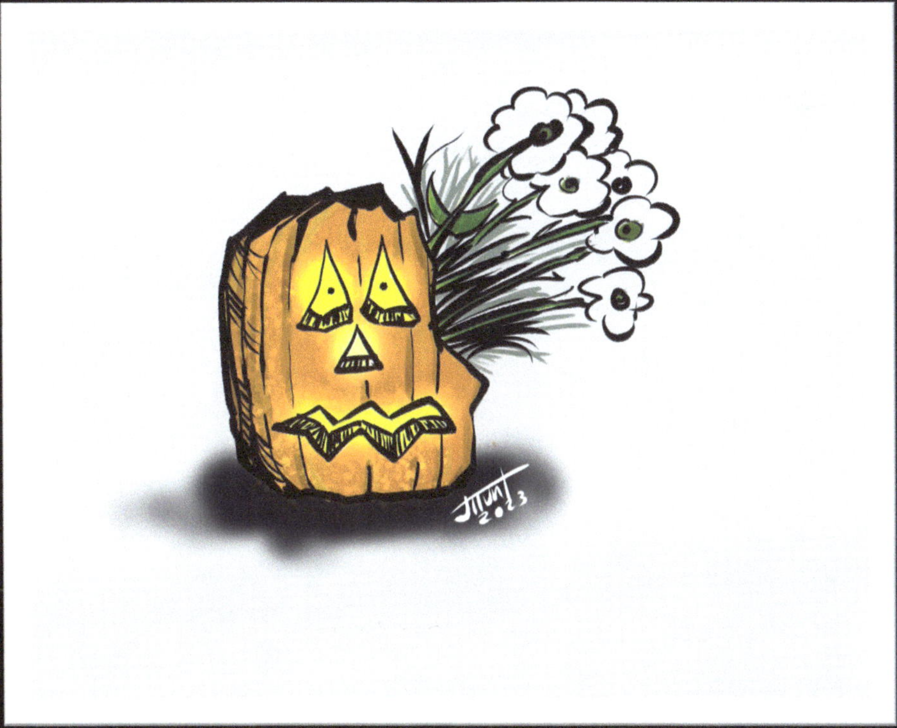

CANDLE PUMPKIN

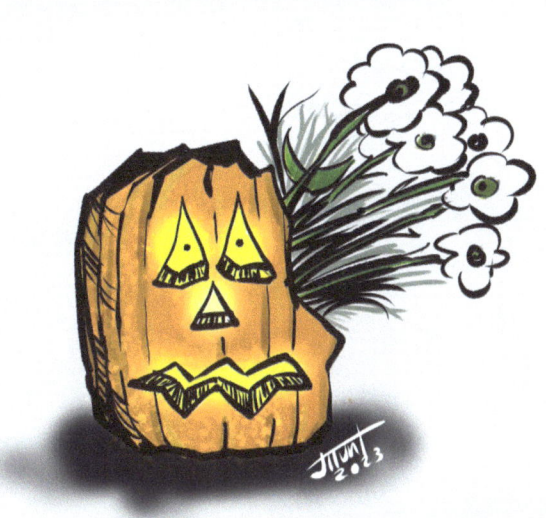

FLOWER PUMPKIN VASE

GHOSTS

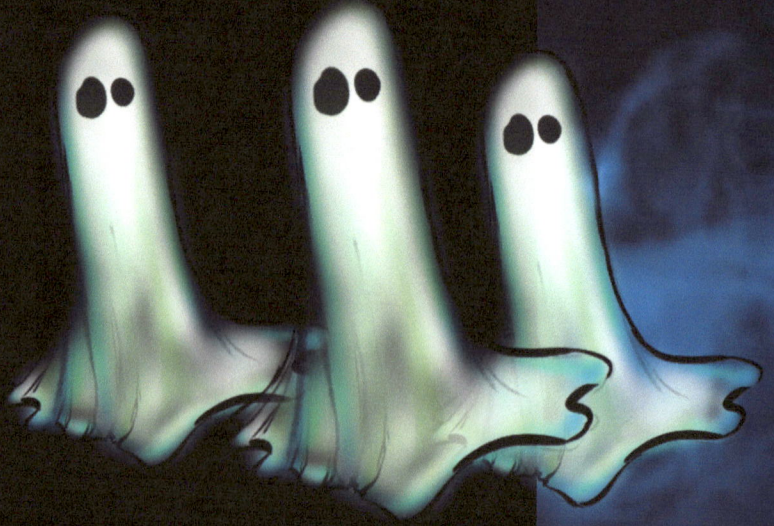

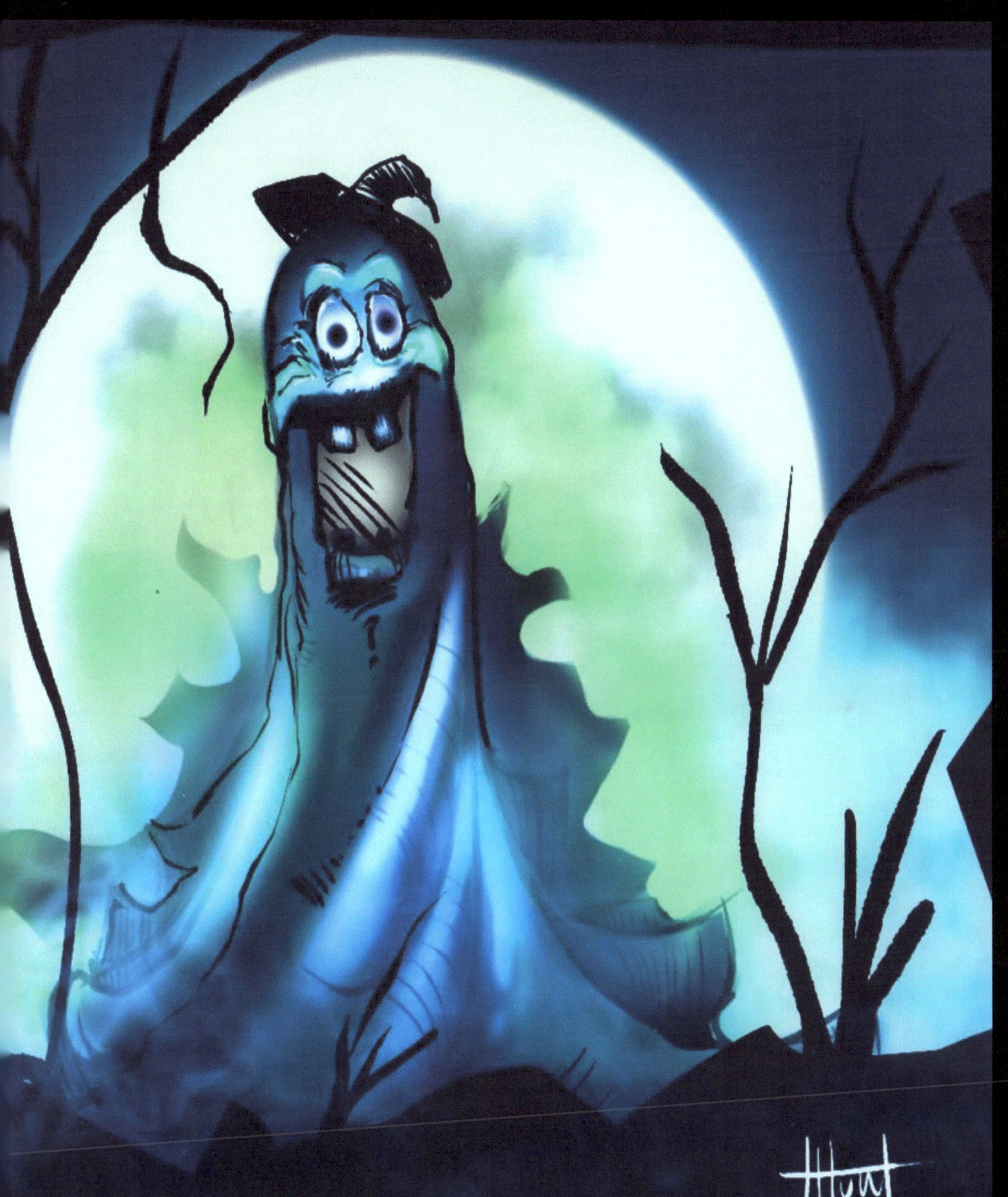

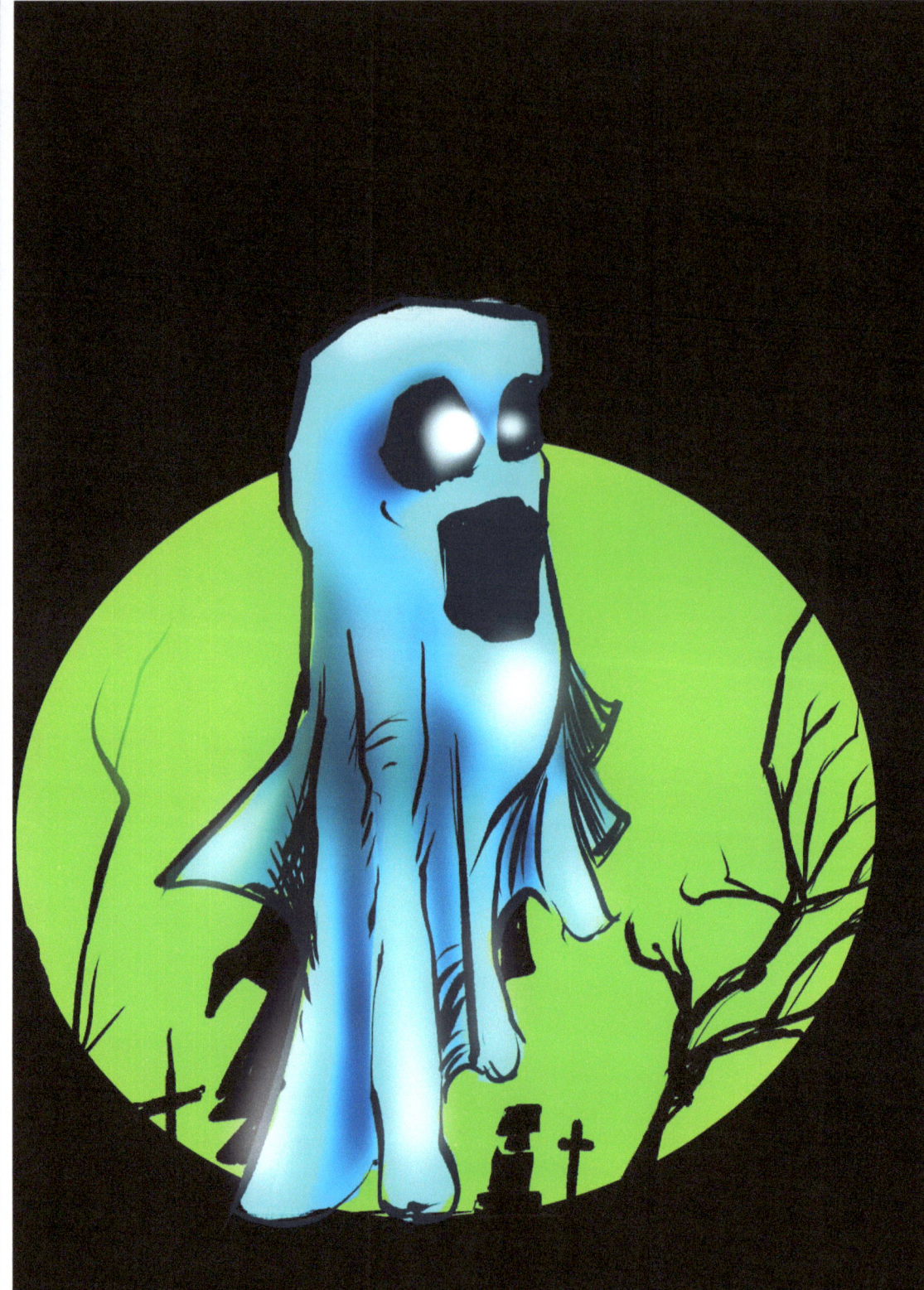

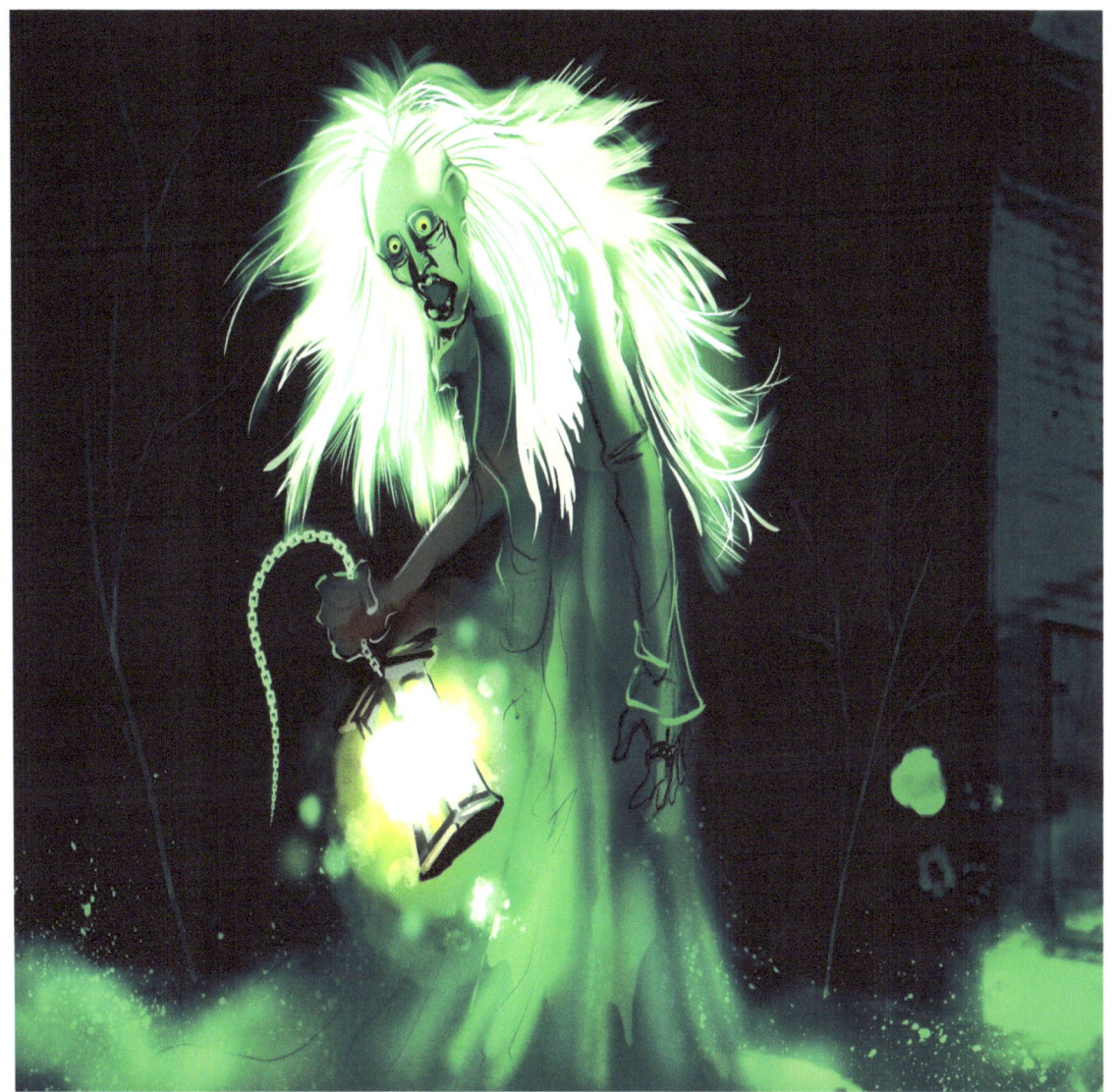

THE CARETAKER

ALSO AVAILABLE

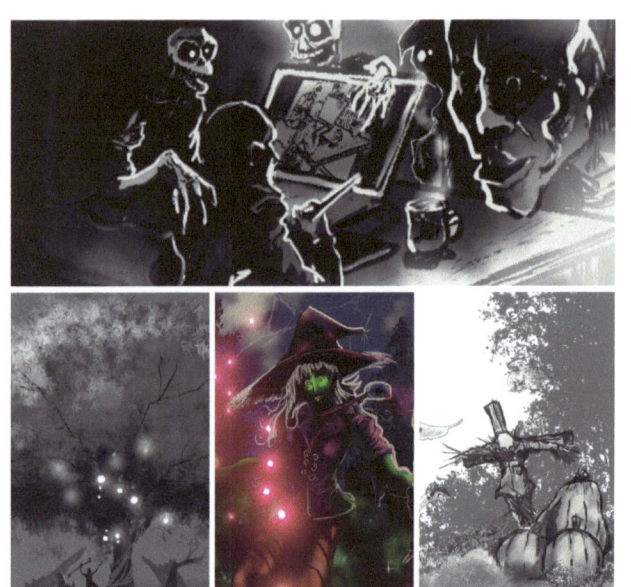
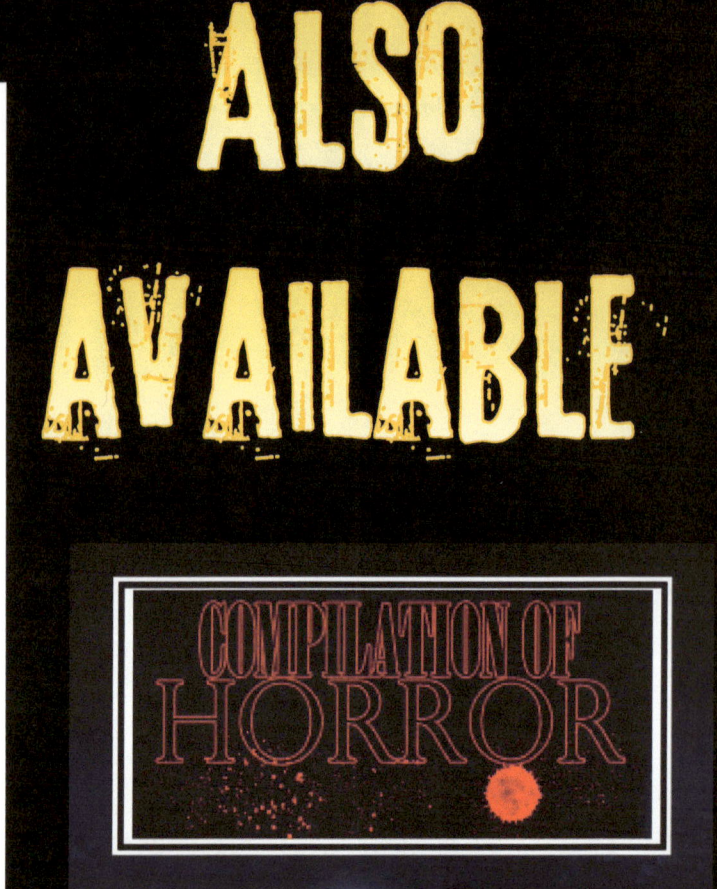
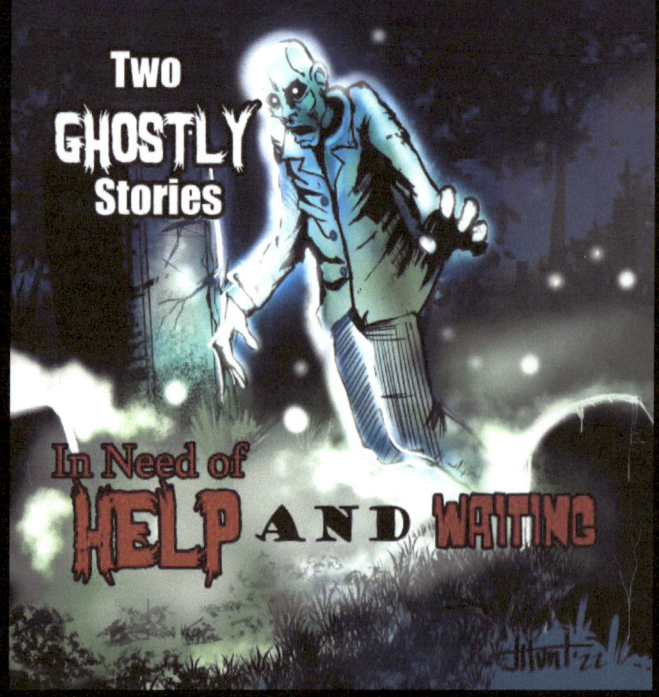

www.ingramcontent.com/pod-product-compliance
Lightning Source LLC
Chambersburg PA
CBHW040455220526
45473CB00004B/1639